Painted Paper

Painted Paper

Techniques & Projects for
Handmade Books & Cards

Alisa Golden

STERLING

New York / London
www.sterlingpublishing.com

STERLING and the distinctive Sterling logo are
registered trademarks of Sterling Publishing Co., Inc.

Library of Congress Cataloging-in-Publication Data Available

2   4   6   8   10   9   7   5   3

Published by Sterling Publishing Co., Inc.
387 Park Avenue South, New York, NY 10016
© 2008 by Alisa Golden
Distributed in Canada by Sterling Publishing
ᶜ/ₒ Canadian Manda Group, 165 Dufferin Street
Toronto, Ontario, Canada M6K 3H6
Distributed in the United Kingdom by GMC Distribution Services
Castle Place, 166 High Street, Lewes, East Sussex, England BN7 1XU
Distributed in Australia by Capricorn Link (Australia) Pty. Ltd.
P.O. Box 704, Windsor, NSW 2756, Australia

Book design and layout by Susan Fazekas
Photographs by Sibila Savage
Chapter calligraphy by Alice Armstrong
Art projects and diagrams by the author

Printed in China

Sterling ISBN-13: 978-1-4027-3193-8
ISBN-10: 1-4027-3193-0

For information about custom editions, special sales, premium and
corporate purchases, please contact Sterling Special Sales
Department at 800-805-5489 or specialsales@sterlingpublishing.com.

contents

preface

PORTALS, 2005; acrylic ink, paint and gesso on paper; 22" × 30" (55.9 cm × 76.2 cm). Techniques: acrylic ink wash, watercolor crayon applied to wet paper, gesso, acrylic paint: *sgraffito*, dropper and dry brush, stencil with acrylic paint

In the 1980s, there was a trend among some painters to cut up a painting, then bind it into a book. I was absorbed in letterpress printing, writing, and making printed books at the time, and didn't give much thought to these painted books.

One letter at a time by hand. That's what setting individual pieces of metal type for letterpress printing was all about for me. It is a detailed and focused activity. Binding books also requires meticulous attention to details. When Anne Schwartzburg (now Stevens) and I decided to collaborate on a letterpress-printed book in 1995, I had no idea that it would lead me into a compelling world of painted paper and painted books.

Anne had been painting paper and writing on top of it for a while, and I liked the look. I chose the title *Tidal Poems*. We decided to paint 120 sheets of paper and then print on top of the painting. I thought that the subject—water and the ocean—would work with the paint.

We spread out ten big white sheets at a time. I paused. Anne jumped in. I picked up a small round brush and slowly made narrow lines. Anne ran around scribbling with paint, making huge circles here, broad washes of color there. As I watched her paint, it occurred to me to follow. I tentatively began imitating her broad gestures. Eventually I became comfortable with the big movements I made and subsequently with the marks they produced. Learning to incorporate this movement into my art-making was one of the most freeing things I had ever done. I could just enjoy the process. Since we planned to cut up all the large sheets into smaller ones to make the book, the process was even more important; we had no idea how each page would turn out. That was another revelation; painted paper that is cut up often looks even better in pieces. As a result, I really liked that the same page of each of the forty copies was different from the others; the printed text hit the paper on different painted spots each time. The type was rigid and formal, the paint was spontaneous and serendipitous.

When the book was complete I wasn't ready to put away the paints. I had some other ideas. The first was a poem about a walk in a Japanese garden. I painted the paper with long, tall grasses like iris leaves and printed the poem on top of it. For this book I devised a binding that would use one large sheet of paper that was cut up, folded into accordions, and joined with archival tape. I called it the Circle Accordion Book, because if you opened up the accordion folds entirely,

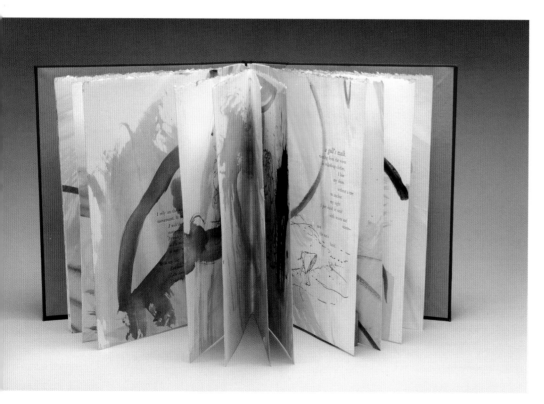

TIDAL POEMS (WITH ANNE SCHWARTZBURG), 1995; letterpress, inks, watercolors, linoleum blocks, photoengravings of drawings by Anne; 10" x 11½" (25.4 cm x 29.2 cm). Technique: acrylic inks applied with a variety of brushes

you would have a circle. Since that time I've made many journals and other books with that format. *Tidal Poems* led to a major change in how I thought about and made my book art. The revelation occurred while watching someone else's process. Once, when I gave a presentation to an art history class, a woman looked at my painted circle accordions, listened to what I had to say about them, and then got very excited. "I've never really done art, but I think I could do that!"

After watching many people paint, I see that each person makes unique marks. Even when someone tries to imitate what I am doing, the result is much more personal. Your painting style is as unique as your own handwriting.

"The night we painted paper I went to bed and slept like a baby," said one woman in class. I had given them blue inks and told them to think of water while they painted. Letting go is part of the process.

WALKING ON THE SENTENCE STONES, 1997; letterpress, acrylic inks, gesso; 5½" × 5" (14 cm × 12.7 cm).
Technique: undiluted acrylic ink applied with a dry brush

SWIM, **2004**; acrylic inks and gesso, ribbon, punched title; 4" × 5¾" (10.2 cm × 14.6 cm). **Techniques:** acrylic ink wash, layered shades of blue with a variety of brushes, stencil with acrylic paint

Acknowledgments

This book is dedicated to Mom, Dad, and my sister Nina. My parents listened when a preschool teacher told them to make sure I always had art lessons. They provided the "art center" in a corner of the family room. It had a ream of newsprint and all kinds of drawing tools, and the "project closet," where we collected orange-juice cans, tomato baskets, yarn, beads, felt, and other craft supplies. My most memorable early art experiences were at Ed and Linda Buttwinick's Brentwood Art Center in Southern California, where I particularly liked a life-drawing class with a costumed model, a watercolor class, and a cartooning class. Thanks to Nina, my first art promoter, who had my work elaborately framed, showcased it wherever she lived, and gave it and sold it to her friends.

For freeing me from rigid painting I want to thank Anne Stevens, who got me on this painting track; I'm extremely grateful I got to paint with her in 1995. I'd also like to acknowledge my former printmaking teacher Ken Rignall at California College of Arts and Crafts (now CCA), who, when I asked what he was doing, replied, "Painting," and when I asked what the subject was, responded, "Anything. It doesn't matter." I am sorry he is no longer with us.

Thanks again to Sibila Savage for the photography; she is truly wonderful to work with, and her work was invaluable for this book. Thanks to Alice Armstrong for the calligraphy and inspiration.

Thanks to all my students; it is always incredible watching you work.

papers, colors & tools

The richness and variety of papers and coloring materials can enhance any project from postcards to books. While you can choose from an endless assortment of preprinted papers, painting them yourself allows you the freedom to experiment with color in fluid form and the satisfaction of knowing that you made them. You have the opportunity to incorporate elements of a theme or story, if you like, or to customize the paper to a specific event or person.

While there are various methods that produce different painted effects, you can combine techniques to create a personal style. Using the examples given in this book, you may choose to create repeating patterns or free-form designs, customized stencils, or translucent layered looks. Just as your signature is different from anyone else's, your painted papers will be unique, capturing your particular style of making marks. You may begin to recognize your own artistic handwriting as you try the variety of techniques that follow in Chapters 2 to 5. After you have painted a variety of papers, you can use them for the books and projects in Chapter 6. The focus of the methods in the middle chapters is on water-based media, primarily acrylic inks and gesso. You can make beautiful and widely varied papers in colors you enjoy with just a few painting methods. Even though I've specifically adapted these techniques for bookmaking projects, the methods are equally good for any paper-based project. To begin, you will need basic supplies such as paper, inks, and brushes. Later, explore gesso and then use it

with stencils you create. Add a masking product, paste, and acrylic paint and you have endless ways to create your own decorated paper. Working with these tools and materials can be relaxing and fun.

Papers and Boards

PAPERS

Each of these papers is useful for different projects and will give a distinctive look to the final product. Very smooth paper, for example, will look more industrial or commercial and modern, while a textured paper adds a handmade character and, possibly, an older appearance. One is not inherently better than the other, but one may add a certain quality to your work that you desire. Sample paper packs are sold in many art-supply stores; getting a pack may be a good, quick, and relatively inexpensive way to look at and try dozens of papers. The papers sold in the packs are a fraction of the size of the parent sheets (original size). Each paper accepts the ink in a different way.

DRIFTWOOD & ROOTS, 2006; acrylic ink, letterpress, linoleum cuts; album accordion; 5¾" x 6¼" (14.6 cm x 15.9 cm).
Technique: layered acrylic inks

ABOUT YOU, 2006; acrylic inks, gesso; circle accordion; 5½" × 6" (14 cm × 15.2 cm). **Techniques:** multicolored droppers and dry brush, stencil with acrylic paint, artist's tape mask

A variety of paper is sold in pads or loose in single sheets. Choose paper by weight, surface texture, and how it will be used. Uses may range from homemade wrapping paper, which would require a soft, lightweight paper that doesn't need to be archival (acid-free), to an accordion-fold book, for which a heavyweight, all-cotton paper is recommended. Loose papers are measured in grams per square meter: the higher the number, the heavier the paper. For the step-by-step photographs, I used *Daniel Smith* or *Legion* Lenox, also called Lenox 100.

Archival Heavyweight Paper (160 to 300 g/m²)

These papers should retain their original colors and not become yellow or turn brittle over decades.
Uses: soft covers, thick pages, accordion-folded books, cards
- *Daniel Smith* or *Legion* Lenox (white)
- *Rising* Stonehenge (tan, black, and whites)

- *Legion* Somerset (radiant white, satin, textured, newsprint)
- 90 -to 140-lb. watercolor paper (115 to 300 g/m²): rough (textured), cold pressed (lightly textured), or hot pressed (smooth)

Archival Textweight Paper (95 to 120 g/m²)

These papers should retain their original colors and not become yellow or turn brittle over decades.
Uses: to wrap boards for hard covers, use as endpapers, stationery, collage
- *Arches* Text Wove, a.k.a. Velin Arches (white)
- *Zerkall* Nideggan (straw-colored)
- *Zerkall* Frankfurt (white or cream)
- *Rives* Lightweight (white or buff)
- *Hahnemuhle* Ingres, a.k.a. German Ingres (variety of colors, including black)
- *Mohawk* or *Daniel Smith* Superfine Text (white, warm white)

Good-Quality Textweight Paper

Commercial papers and papers in pads are usually labeled in pounds. Generally, the higher the number, the heavier the paper. These papers should last a few years.

Uses: some books, wrapping paper, backing for art exhibits or window displays, collage

- Multipurpose paper (24-lb. copier or printer paper)
- *Strathmore* 400 Drawing Paper (white) or other 70-lb. drawing paper
- *Canson* Sketch Paper (50-lb.)
- Maps

BOARDS

Museum Boards

All cotton and acid-free, these boards are usually used for picture framing. They come in four-ply and two-ply and are found in most art-supply stores. They are soft and fairly easy to cut with a standard art knife.

The four-ply ($\frac{1}{16}$" or 1.7 mm) is recommended for most bookmaking purposes; it may require a new blade or multiple strokes to cut all the way through. Since this board comes in white and off-white, it can be painted on directly with good results.

Davey Board

Also known as book board or binder's board, this is a high-quality buffered board made of sulphite pulp, which comes in various thicknesses. A good weight for books less than 10 inches in either direction (25 cm) is 1.7 millimeters thick, which is approximately the equivalent of a four-ply museum board. Board thicker than this can be very difficult to cut. You will need a heavier knife, such as a utility knife. Davey board thickness is also given as a caliper size, which is measured with a micrometer to 1,000th of an inch; one caliper point is equal to .001 inch.

***FALLING OUT OF BED PURPLE,* 2006;** acrylic inks, acrylic paints, gesso, letterpress printing from metal and wood type; 3⅜" × 3½" (7.8 cm × 8.9 cm).

Techniques: acrylic ink wash, handwriting, gesso resist, acrylic-painted covers

DRYING
WET PAPER

Wet paper has a natural tendency to curl, especially if it is painted on only one side. The best way to keep your paper flat is to paint on both sides of the paper or, for bookmaking, paint one side and use glue on the other. There are times when you'll want to paint just on one side or to make stacks of paper and you don't have space to dry them. Paste papers, in particular, take a long time to dry. You could use a hair dryer, you could put them out in the sun, or you could make your own drying rack.

I use a hair dryer set on high heat, low air. It takes about five minutes to dry the paper this way.

On a sunny day, clothespins on a line work fine, so does a wooden laundry drying rack. If you have pieces of cardboard larger than your paper, you can clip the paper to the board with binder clips and put it out in the sun.

You can improvise a drying rack if you have large pieces of cardboard and a dozen or more paper cups or yogurt containers. Place one cup (open side down) at each corner of a piece of cardboard. Balance another piece of cardboard on top of the cups and repeat, making a stacking sandwich. Put one piece of your painted paper on each level.

Techniques: acrylic ink wash over gesso resist, marble effect, stencil with gold gesso, acrylic ink lettering applied with a ruling pen

Ultimately, your climate may affect how flat a paper treated only on one side will dry. For example, when I take books made in the foggy San Francisco Bay Area to the more desertlike climate of Los Angeles, they tend to warp. When I bring them back, they relax. They also will likely warp if you leave them in a hot car. Changes in humidity affect all papers.

Some Davey-board thicknesses and approximate equivalents:
- 1.7 mm, .067 caliper, $^1/_{16}$", or 68 pt.
- 1.9 mm, .074 caliper, $^5/_{64}$" (slightly between $^1/_{16}$" and $^1/_8$") or 74 pt.
- 2.1 mm, .082 caliper, $^3/_{32}$", or 80 pt.

Illustration Board

Look for boards that say all-cotton (or rag) and acid-free. Some have a backing sheet that is not acid-free. Over time, such boards will yellow or begin to turn spotty (this is known as foxing).

Inks, Paints, and Other Media

Inks, paints, gesso, and paste have distinctive characteristics that make them good for use in certain situations and not useful in others. They may be thick and gel-like or fluid and runny. They may stay tacky or they may dry to a smooth finish. Each technique shown in the following chapters uses a specific medium. Unless the instructions call for it, another medium cannot be substituted with the same results.

After trying out a variety of watercolor and illustration inks to create the book *Tidal Poems* with my friend Anne, I stumbled upon the acrylic inks ten years ago and have stuck with them ever since. The majority of the techniques in this book are done with acrylic inks. I like the variety of colors and how they dry smooth and not at all tacky; this is great for bookmaking, because pages painted with the inks won't stick together. Additionally, you can use watercolor crayons to draw into an ink-painted paper while it is still wet.

Acrylic paint applied thickly straight out of the tube or jar may not work well for book pages, but using it sparingly or mixing it with other media can expand its uses. It works well for stenciling, for example, either when used in small amounts or when mixed with gesso, because the addition of gesso reduces the stickiness of the paint. Stenciling requires a thick medium so that the color doesn't leak under the edges of the image. Both the gesso and the acrylic paint are relatively stiff and work well for this purpose. Acrylic paint added to paste gives a nice color, look, and feel to paste papers. The paste keeps the paint wet longer, which leaves you time to draw, scrape, wipe away, and redraw into the paint for another interesting layered and textured effect.

Technique: Example of ink pencils over paste paper (top) and painted paper (bottom)

PIGMENTS AND DYES

In a papermaking class in college I learned that pigments and dyes are not the same. A pigment generally remains a powder, can be mixed with a liquid, but does not dissolve. Acrylic inks are pigmented and therefore need to be shaken every time you use them. A dye generally refers to a color that is soluble in liquid: neither shaking nor stirring is needed. Often when people talk about pigments they are also talking about a color that is permanent or lightfast/fadeproof. A dye-based ink is considered fugitive—meaning that it fades easily. Look for inks or paints that are labeled "lightfast" and "pigmented." These colors are less likely to fade over time. Certain colors will fade more quickly than others even if they are pigments. Reds and oranges are two examples. Browns are highly lightfast. Therefore, even when using pigmented products it is best to keep your finished papers out of direct sunlight to preserve their bright colors.

If you are trying to match colors, be aware that color names may vary between inks and paints. The ink "red earth" may match a paint called "red oxide" but just have a different name. And paints with the same name from different brands may also not match. If you want to match the colors shown in the examples given, use *Daler-Rowney* FW acrylic inks and *Golden* acrylic paints.

Once the papers are dry, you have additional options to further develop your idea or enhance your project. You can change the way the papers feel by sanding, waxing, or varnishing. You can add more color by drawing on top of the papers with ink pencils, then brushing over the marks with a wet brush to activate the colors. Although they have the word "ink" in their name, the ink pencils look like regular graphite pencils and function similarly to watercolor pencils. Using rubber stamps is another way to add imagery.

ACRYLIC INKS

While browsing the aisles of an art-supply store, you will likely come across a wide range of inks; look for inks that specifically say "acrylic" and "lightfast." These versatile inks can be used straight out of the bottle or diluted with water. You can also mix them together for custom colors. Because the inks are permanent, once they are dry you can layer more inks on top of them and the colors will still remain vibrant. As long as each layer is dry before another is added, they won't blend or become muddy. This layering is also called glazing, especially when the layers are thin or transparent.

Within the acrylic-ink community there are two varieties, a regular color and a pearlescent one, and both may be used. The regular colors are formulated to be either opaque or transparent. Opaque colors will hide the layer below. Transparent colors let the previous layer show through them; they're nice for adding depth. Try experimenting with both kinds. The pearlescent inks have bits of shimmery, light-reflective material in them that make them look glittery; these are all transparent.

Cleanup for acrylic ink is easy—just soap and water—as long as it is still wet. Be sure to clean the brushes and containers before the ink dries. Once it is

I WANT IT, 2007; variety of painted paper and paste paper, beads, velvet, linen thread; 5" × 4½" × 1½" (12.7 cm × 11.4 cm × 3.8 cm) box, 2" × 2½" × 1¼" (5.1 cm × 6.4 cm × 3.2 cm) book.
Techniques: wash, wet-on-wet, layered freehand forms, gesso and handcut stencils, paste paper frottage

dry, the ink will make your brushes stiff and unusable. Warm water and soap will take ink off of your hands, though, even if the ink has dried.

Other inks you may see are watercolor, shellac-based, and dye-based, and they may refer to a medium such as drawing, calligraphy, or illustration. The acrylic-ink labels may also refer to drawing or illustration, but the fact that they are acrylic-based and lightfast is the important part.

Most of the projects in this book are made with FW inks. They come in a wide variety of colors and are readily available. Results will vary slightly depending on the brand of ink you choose. For comparison of colors and consistencies, I chose purple from four brands since each brand only offered one shade of purple, and tried them out, making the comparison chart you see here. The FW and the Design Higgins inks were fairly thin. The *Speedball* and *Tri Art* inks were much thicker. The *Speedball*, in particular, took longer to dry when it wasn't mixed with water. The comparison chart shows that the colors were different from one another, even though all were designated purple. Try different brands or dilute the inks to find the ink consistencies and colors you prefer. If you live in Australia, *Matisse* inks, which are only available there (and not shown in the photo), are similar to the FW.

Varieties of acrylic inks

As an alternative to ink, try thinning acrylic paint with water to a creamy consistency: the color selection is endless. The paints will be transparent and work well for glazing (layering or stacking the colors.) See page 30 for the acrylic paint glaze recipe. The only colors that don't work well when thinned are black and white. I recommend black and white inks instead because they are opaque. Using white and black inks to write or draw on top of painted paper after it dries makes a highly legible mark.

Here are some common acrylic ink brands available in various countries:

United States and United Kingdom: FW Acrylic by *Daler-Rowney* (they also make Calli inks), Design Higgins Fadeproof inks by *Sanford, Speedball* Superpigmented Acrylic inks

Australia: *Matisse/Derivan* makes Matisse inks and Derivan inks (thicker)

Canada: *Tri Art* Acrylic Ink (can also be used on fabric and leather)

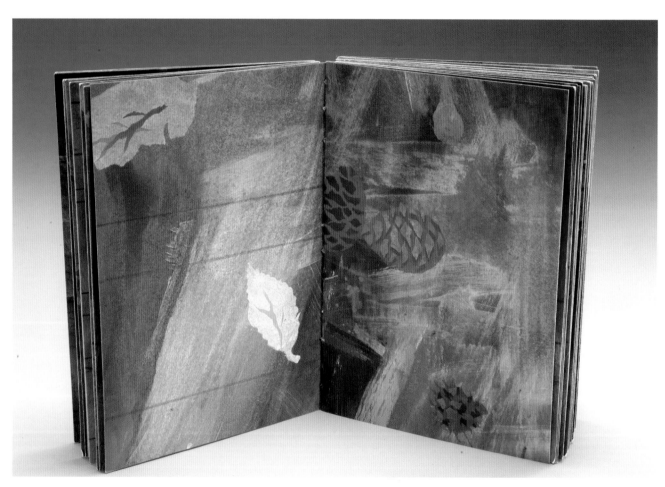

FALL VISION, 2004; acrylic inks, gesso, stencil, graphite; Coptic binding; 5" x 7" (12.7 cm x 17.8 cm).
Techniques: acrylic ink wash, gesso: sgraffito, multicolored hand-cut stencils with Venetian red gesso, acrylic inks mixed with white gesso, gold gesso, pencil

CHOOSING COLORS

Acrylics behave differently when they are wet than when dry. Wet colors next to each other on paper will mingle spontaneously, or you can mix them yourself ahead of time. In each case, once the mixed colors dry they become permanent. You won't be able to move them around anymore, and they will not mix with other colors. Choose your colors carefully, so they either blend or layer as you desire.

Complementary colors when mixed wet will produce brown. The complementary colors are purple/yellow, green/red, and orange/blue. Other wet colors mixed together produce specific third colors: red/yellow (orange), yellow/blue (green), or blue/red (purple). Within a single color group, such as blue, several hues—turquoise, Prussian, cobalt, for example—can be used together wet to make other shades for a graduated wash or to indicate depth.

Once the colors are dry you can layer more color on top of or next to them without any color mixing. Complementary colors enhance each other, each making the other look bolder; for example, orange lines and blue lines next to each other seem to pop brightly off the page. Once colors are dry you can use other color layers to shade some areas or to add pattern, texture, or text. You might add splatters of silver, gold, or pearlescent color for a decorative look. Try using transparent colors to shade an area or make it recede. Writing with opaque colors on top of the painted paper works particularly well. Experiment with different brushes to enhance the layered, textured look.

Certain color combinations will likely appeal to you more than others. Make a note of your favorites. These colors are often based on colors you choose for your clothes and the dominant colors in the news for home and fashion. Those are the surface colors; they are obvious and appealing in an instant. You may also base color on the nature of your specific project. If your subject is plants, for example, you would likely choose shades of green. Who is your audience or gift recipient? What colors do they like? Think about the colors they wear. You might add these colors to your palette.

One student kept looking at my papers and asking how I did something, saying she didn't want to "reinvent the wheel." I showed her my techniques but encouraged her to enjoy herself and play with the materials. Try exploring with wet inks and layering over dry areas. The following chapters contain examples how you might begin so you don't have to reinvent the wheel; you will likely stumble upon something new just by experimenting. Begin with three colors: a light one, a medium color, and a dark one, or choose three related colors, such as shiny gold, yellow ochre, and burnt umber.

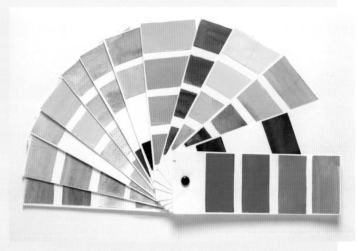

Homemade color chart

***I TRIED MAKING FRIENDS WITH NUMBERS*, 2005;** acrylic inks, watercolor crayons; Coptic binding; 5¼" × 6" (13.4 cm × 15.2 cm).
Techniques: acrylic ink wash, watercolor crayon applied to wet paper

ACRYLIC PAINTS

Acrylic paints are water-based and dry quickly. Undiluted, they are opaque; they cover the surface completely. You can paint over previously painted areas and the underlayer won't show through. They can be transparent if you add another medium or extender to them, such as water, paste, or acrylic gel medium. Because the paint dries fast, you don't have to wait before adding more color, but you will have to keep your brushes wet or rinse them as soon as you are finished so you can keep the bristles soft and supple.

Acrylic paints are useful in small amounts for stenciling (Chapter 3), making paste papers (Chapter 5), and painting directly on boards for book covers.

Using the paint straight from the tube for stenciling is fine, or you can mix it with gesso for a tinted matte finish. The paints are also useful alone or in combination with other acrylic media to paint on paper that is intended to stay flat, such as postcards or artwork to be mounted or framed.

Acrylic paints are sold under different brand names. Each brand has its own properties; some are creamier, some are thicker. You may want to experiment until you find the one you like best. Iridescent and metallic varieties are also available. Small amounts are sold in tubes, large quantities are sold in jars or tubs. All brands work equally well for the techniques in this book.

WATERCOLOR CRAYONS

Watercolor crayons are creamy, smooth, and intense, and allow you to draw solid lines. They are also useful for handwriting, as shown in the book in the photo on the facing page. I don't recommend watercolor pencils; they tend to dig into wet paper and leave a dent, sometimes tearing the paper. Watercolor crayons are sold individually or in sets with a huge variety of colors. Even with the availability of so many terrific colors, however, my students and I tend to use the black most often. These crayons may, of course, be used dry as well as with plain wet paper or with a colored wash. Although the colors may rub off when used alone, if you loosen the pigment on the page with water or paint an acrylic wash or varnish over them, the colors will lock into place.

GESSO

Gesso (pronounced jess-o) is commonly used as a canvas primer. The paintlike substance is brushed over the surface of the canvas to make it nonabsorbent. For our applications, however, we don't need to prime the paper, since the paper has the perfect degree of absorbency. Gesso does have specific qualities, though, that are useful for painted-paper techniques. It is a good consistency for stenciling and it can be added to acrylic paint so the paint dries with a matte finish instead of remaining tacky; the matte finish will prevent book pages or folded cards from sticking together.

The whiteness of most gessos comes from the addition of titanium white, although some vendors, such as Daniel Smith, have been able to formulate gessos in dark colors. Instead of white, they use a

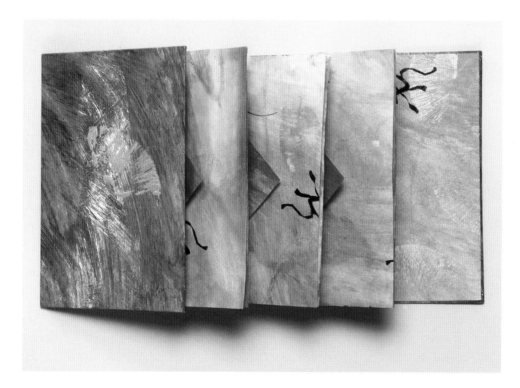

Techniques: acrylic ink applied with various brushes, gesso, handmade stencils, dropper and dry brush, fan brush marks with gold gesso

different pigment. While you can mix regular acrylic paint with the common white gesso for stenciling or for a matte finish, you will be limited to light tints only. Available colors of full-color, pre-made gesso, as of this writing, are black, gray, red, brown, metallic gold, and yellow. When it is dry the gold works particularly well as an underlayer beneath paste paper frottage (page 107).

Gesso is sold in bottles and jars. I've found that gesso in a bottle has a nicer texture when dry but is too runny to use with stencils. Gesso in a jar has a thicker consistency, which is good for stenciling.

Different brands of gesso are grittier than others when dry; you may want to experiment with them. Try rubbing beeswax over the finished surface to smooth any rough spots (see "Waxed Finish," page 116).

WHEAT PASTE AND METHYLCELLULOSE

Both of these pastes begin as powders that are then mixed with water. Instructions for making paste papers and recipes for the pastes are included in Chapter 5. After it is mixed, either wheat paste or methylcellulose may also be mixed with acrylic paint to change the

PAINTED PAPER SAMPLER,
2006; variety of painted papers; 4½" × 5⅜" (11.4 cm × 13.3 cm).
Techniques: paste papers, acrylic ink–painted papers, collage on paste paper background

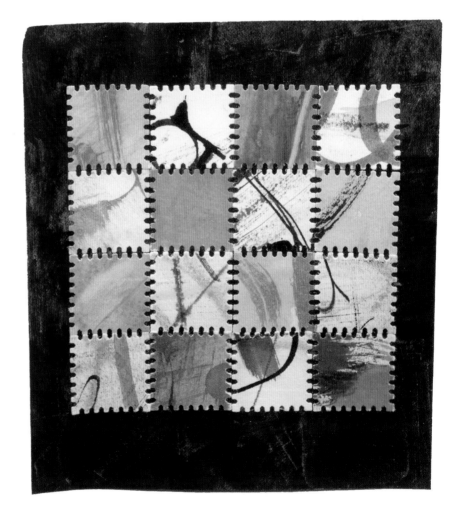

**DECEPTION: JACOB'S VOICE,
2006;** molding paste with
embedded objects, acrylic
paints, acrylic inks, museum
board; album accordion; 3½" ×
6" (8.9 cm × 15.2 cm).
Techniques: acrylic paints over
texture paints for the cover; dry
brush and dropper, acrylic ink
wash, layered acrylic inks for the
pages

paint's consistency and to allow it to stay wet longer (also known as "open" time). The advantage to a longer open time is that you can then draw into the wet painted paper with a stick to make free-form shapes or use a texturing tool (such as a comb) to incise patterns. You can also wipe the drawings or patterns away easily and start again. Some people call the making of paste papers "finger painting for grown-ups," but it is a historical paper-decorating technique, long used in bookbinding. Paste alone or a paste/paint mixture is also good for collage.

TEXTURE PASTE

Texture paste is versatile. It is already mixed and can be a stand-in for the paste used in paste papers or it can be used alone to create a thick, raised surface for a book cover like *Deception: Jacob's Voice,* in the photograph above. It is a kind of acrylic gel medium

that holds deeper, wider grooves than other pastes. It is somewhat flexible by nature, but when used undiluted and applied thickly to thin paper, it may peel or crack.

If you use texture paste and then paint over it with acrylic paint, the color will remain opaque. You may also mix ink or paint with the paste before applying it, which will produce a translucent, somewhat luminous effect. In this way the paste stretches the color, diluting it.

This paste is easy to use and mix with acrylic paints for paste papers, but once it is thinned out it dries more quickly than the other pastes. If you have a limited amount of time to work on a project, using texture paste will give you more time to cut up the paper and create the project with it right away.

Texture paste comes in a jar, premixed, and looks like a thick, milky acrylic paint. It keeps forever. You can find it at art-supply stores, labeled either "molding

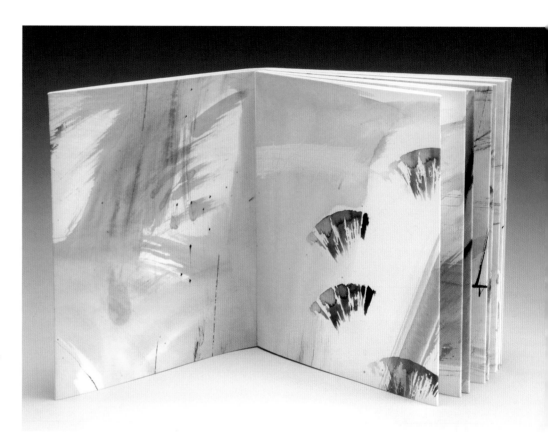

Techniques: acrylic ink wash, watercolor crayon, gesso, acrylic paint: sgraffito, dropper and dry brush, stencil with acrylic paint

paste" or "modeling paste." You may also use other kinds of acrylic gel medium, if you like; the final product will be fairly durable.

Brushes

In general, all you need for acrylic media are synthetic brushes of any shape and size. When you're shopping, you'll see size is indicated by number: the higher the number, the bigger the brush. Additionally, start with some inexpensive house-painting brushes (a kind of wash brush) with any sort of soft bristles in sizes from 1" to 3" (2.5 cm to 7.6 cm) wide. It's good to have a variety of brushes; combined strokes from different kinds of brushes give depth and texture to the finished piece.

Here are the styles of brushes used for the techniques included in this book. See the

recommended sizes and the types of strokes each makes in the photo on the facing page:

Round. Gives a controlled line. A large round brush (#16 or #20) is good for broad strokes and roughing in broad shapes; a child's brush works for this also. Small round brushes (#8 to #12) are good for narrow strokes, lines, and details; you can also use a child's tiny round watercolor brush or a small round sumi brush, such as gyokuran. A mop brush is a large round brush that can hold a generous quantity of water, ink, or paint; it doesn't need to be loaded as frequently as smaller brushes.

Flat. A stiff brush that gives an even line. One that is ½" to 1" (1.3 cm to 2.5 cm) is good for roughing in shapes with straight sides and making flat strokes in

Brushes (left to right): child's small watercolor round, #10 artist's round, child's large round, small wash brush, medium wash brush, large wash brush, artist's deerfoot brush, small stencil brush, medium stencil brush, artist's fan brush

confined areas. Dedicate one ½" (1.3 cm) flat brush to liquid masking fluid.

Wash. Provides color for large areas. Also used dry to smooth out wet spots and for a specific dry-brush look. Use a 1" (2.5 cm) wash brush to make flat strokes for confined areas; a 1½" to 2" (3.8 cm to 5.1 cm) brush to make flat strokes for large areas; and a 3" (7.6 cm) brush to make flat strokes for overall color.

Stencil. Allows control and even application. This very specific kind of brush is cylindrical with a flat bottom. The bristles are generally short so that they do not

absorb much paint, which is desirable when stenciling. You can also use them without stencils to make circles on the page; just use the brush in an up-and-down stamping motion instead of a side-to-side brushing one. It's good to have several sizes, ranging from approximately ½" to 1" (1.3 cm to 2.5 cm) in diameter.

Fan. Gives interesting shapes. Use (any size: mine is #8) for animal tracks, flowers, curvy washes, or just for triangular textures. If you are painting for the first time, try experimenting with a fan brush. Since it does not look like a conventional brush you may find that you feel free to use it more creatively.

BRUSH CARE

Always rinse your brushes immediately after use to keep the bristles soft and supple. Acrylic media are made of a kind of plastic that hardens permanently, which is unkind to a brush. When washing out a stencil brush, rinse, squeeze the bristles, and rinse again. Repeat this process until the water runs clear when you squeeze the bristles. To preserve their ends or tips, keep all brushes in a jar with the bristle-ends up, or roll the brushes in a mat made especially for brush storage.

Other Marking Tools

In addition to using brushes, there are other ways to make marks on paper for decoration and expression. You can use conventional color-dispensing tools such as watercolor crayons, pencils, and markers, or you can dip objects like string and sticks into the inks and paints and then use them for different effects. Stamping is another markmaking activity. The tools you choose and how you use them to make marks contribute to your individual style. Your finished product will be unique.

Techniques: acrylic inks applied with various brushes, watercolor crayon dipped in water applied to dry paper, brush-handle painting

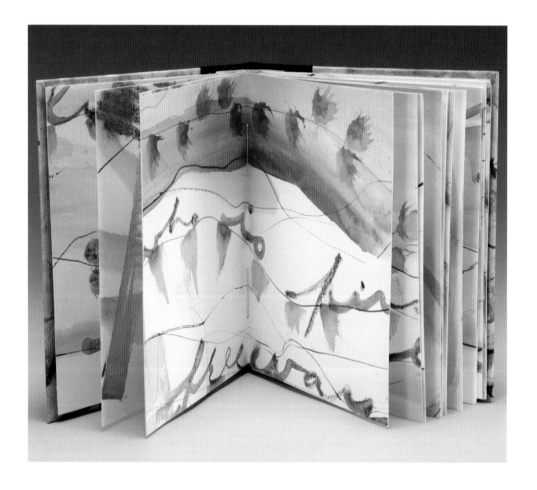

As soon as we pick up a tool, we impose our personality on it. How we hold it has an impact on what we make with it. Although we all learned how to write the letters of the alphabet and probably looked at a standardized, printed version to do so, each person's handwriting is different from the next person's. Unless you are doing a paint-by-numbers kit, your work will be different from another reader's and from mine. Here is a chance to find out what kinds of marks you like. Begin by exploring a few tools.

If you have an adventurous spirit you will naturally look around and try dipping various objects in ink and seeing what marks they make. If you are not sure which things to try, you'll find some examples on the following page of tools and their marks. If you find brushes intimidating, start by playing with unconventional items. Fill a small, shallow paper or plastic cup with black or a dark color of acrylic or any kind of ink, so the ink just covers the bottom of the cup. If you have to dip too deeply into the cup, use a scissors and trim the cup to 1" (5.1 cm) high. Add more ink as needed.

PAINTING SUPPLIES

In addition to brushes and markmaking tools, have the following items on hand when you paint—they'll make the process smooth and tidy. They are listed in order of importance.

APRON. Wear an apron to protect your clothes; acrylic inks and paint are permanent.

WATER CONTAINERS. Small, clean, food-storage containers or plastic cups work well.

PLASTIC OR VINYL TABLECLOTH. To protect your work surface.

PAPER TOWELS. To blot excess ink or paint and for cleanup.

SPRAY BOTTLE. Fill it with water and use to mist paper before adding ink or paint.

KITCHEN SPONGES. To help dampen paper before adding ink or paint.

DISPOSABLE LATEX GLOVES. Protect your hands by wearing thin latex gloves—you can purchase them in bulk at a beauty- or medical-supply store.

CONTAINERS WITH LIDS. Clean, empty food-storage containers are ideal for storing mixed inks and paints.

PAPER PLATES OR PAINTER'S PALETTE. For mixing paint colors or gesso or paste with paint.

DRYING RACK. You can easily make a rack (page 12) for drying multiple sheets of paper. Or just make sure you have a flat surface large enough for whatever you're painting.

BLOW DRYER. Optional, but handy to speed the drying process, especially when you are working with pastes.

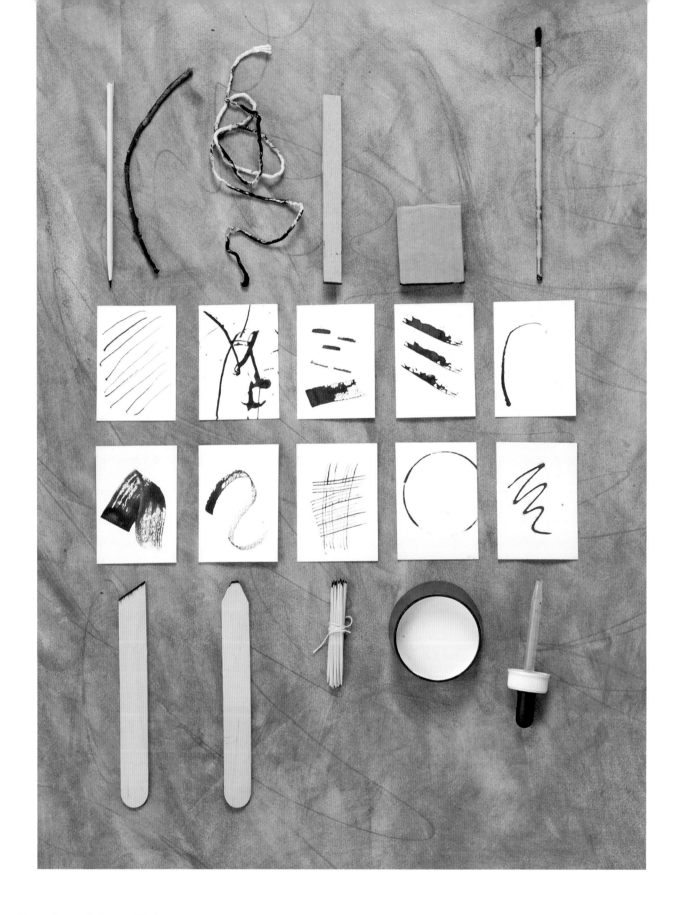

Sticks or skewers. Make lines until the ink runs out, then dip again and either continue the line or start a new one.

String. Dip the string in the cup, then pull it out by one end and drag it across the paper. Try coiling it and stamping with it.

Piece of cardboard. Dip one end, then press the end onto the paper. Try again by changing the angle of the cardboard. Also try dragging the cardboard across the page. Corrugated cardboard leaves an interesting mark.

Brush handle. Hold a small round brush by its bristles. Dip the handle in the ink and make lines with the handle, dipping in ink as the line disappears. See this technique used on page 46.

Sharpened tongue depressor or craft stick. Use a utility knife and cut off the rounded end of the stick on a diagonal. Dip the stick into the ink and try marking with this broad, flat, cut side. Turn the stick as you mark, making thick and thin lines.

Bundle of toothpicks. Tie a small fistful of toothpicks together. Dip them in ink and make marks with the ends.

Cup. Pour a little ink on a plastic lid. Dip the bottom of a cup into the ink and stamp with it, making rings on the paper.

Dropper tip. Some inks come with a dropper tip. Fill the tip by pinching the bulb first to squeeze the air out. Keeping the bulb pinched, put the tip in a deep pool of ink. Gently release the bulb as the dropper fills. Use the filled tip like a pen, writing a word in cursive or making circles and lines. Use a dry-wash brush, paper towel, or blow through a straw to move any large puddles. Refill the dropper frequently. See this technique on page 42. For bottles without dropper tips, you can use a glass pipette (available at scientific tool and supply houses) or a drug store medicine dropper.

Markmaking implements
Top row (left to right): sticks, string, cardboard, corrugated cardboard, brush handle
Bottom row (left to right): angled flat craft stick, tapered flat craft stick, toothpick bundle, cup, dropper tip

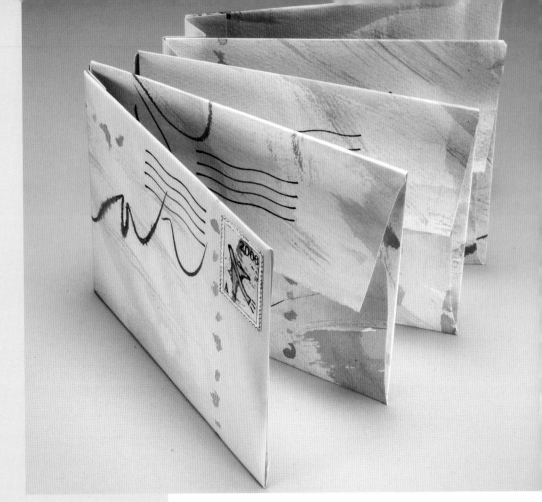

AIR MAIL, 2006; acrylic inks, rubber stamps; single-flag accordion binding; 5¾" × 4¼" (14.6 cm × 10.4 cm).
Techniques: acrylic ink wash, acrylic ink applied with various brushes, multicolored droppers and dry brush, rubber stamps, hand-carved rubber stamp airplane

2 *acrylic inks*

Fluid and bright, acrylic inks can be used to create background washes or expressive layered effects. The layering quality, in particular, is what distinguishes the inks from other media. Acrylic inks have a special property that allows you to layer the colors, painting one over another, each layer remaining bright and clear. These layers and underlayers are like veils, each adding visual texture and depth to the final piece. Images may appear to be in the foreground or

PHARAOH'S DAUGHTER,
2006; pearlescent acrylic
inks, linoleum cuts,
letterpress ox-plow book
in pyramid box; 6" square ×
6" tall (15.2 cm × 15.2 cm ×
15.2 cm).
Technique: acrylic ink wash

recede and hide mysteriously, softly shaded by the colors above them. This type of layering works only when you let one color dry before adding the next one. Using a blow dryer helps speed up the already quick drying time.

By using one color or a selection of colors, then letting them dry, you can create an underlayer for many kinds of effects. For example, you can experiment with inks to simulate wood grain and marble. You can also use black for outlines, then fill in with a brilliant color straight from the bottle to get the look of stained glass, as described in the section on dropper and dry-brush technique (page 42). Note that concentrated pools of color remain tacky to the touch

even when they are dry, so be sure the ink is moved around, blotted, or flattened out. For varied line widths and the suggestion of movement, use a dry brush to move any wet lines or brushstrokes aside. For controlled lines, dip the brushes directly into the ink, paint, then blot carefully with a paper towel.

You can create layers of acrylic inks by using inks straight from the bottle or diluted with water for background underlayers or top shading. Since you can mix them while they are still wet, you can prepare and create custom colors in a cup in advance or use the inks on wet paper to blend them spontaneously as you paint. For softer shades, you can also dilute them with water for a wash.

RECIPE FOR ACRYLIC PAINT GLAZE

You can use this solution for any technique calling for acrylic ink. Once acrylic paints are diluted and dry, they will not stick to each other or to your furniture. The recipe calls for distilled water, which is preferable for archival use

- ½ ounce (15 ml) distilled water
- 5 inches (12.5 cm) acrylic paint from a tube
- 1-ounce (29.5 ml) bottle or other small container with lid

Rinse the bottle thoroughly. Add distilled water. Squeeze the paint into the water. Stir or shake well. Use a separate container for each color.

CREATING "OLD" PAGES

Use layers of acrylic inks to "age" the paper, suggesting a history or story behind it. Begin by creating a wash of diluted yellow ochre or raw sienna. After the painted paper is dry, add a wash of antelope brown or sepia, darkening the color at the edges. For extra depth, finish with a third wash of Prussian blue, varying the shade of the color across the page. Try this effect over found papers, such as the envelopes in the book seen here, *First Class*.

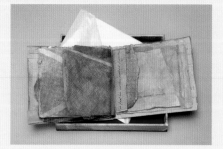

When working on damp paper, such as for the wash techniques, you can still add color layers, but the colors will spread and blend. This blending is desirable, especially when you want one color to merge seamlessly into another creating a graduated wash. Note in the photo, on page 29, how the pearlescent colors (hot mama) red and the (mazuma) gold in *Pharaoh's Daughter* blend to produce an orange where they meet and give a shimmering, desert effect. When working with a lot of water, the fibers in some soft papers tend to roll up, forming little pills—not an effect you want. You can avoid this by painting gently and trying not to spend too much time on one area, or you can buy paper particularly suited to working wet. Watercolor paper is sized, or specially treated to withstand lots of liquid and firm or multiple brushstrokes in one area. I'd recommend watercolor paper if you become fond of the wet-on-wet techniques.

Additional media can be used to add content or a theme to your painted paper. Rubber stamps, for example, can provide focal points for smaller projects or patterned wrappings. Watercolor crayons can be used to draw on a wash or add words to a paper while it is still wet. Black or white acrylic ink used with a crow quill pen works well to write messages or poems on a painted paper that has dried.

Painting with acrylic inks can be both relaxing and exciting at the same time, especially if you use the large wash brushes or work quickly. You can capture your movements in color.

For more details about acrylic inks, see Chapter 1, page 14.

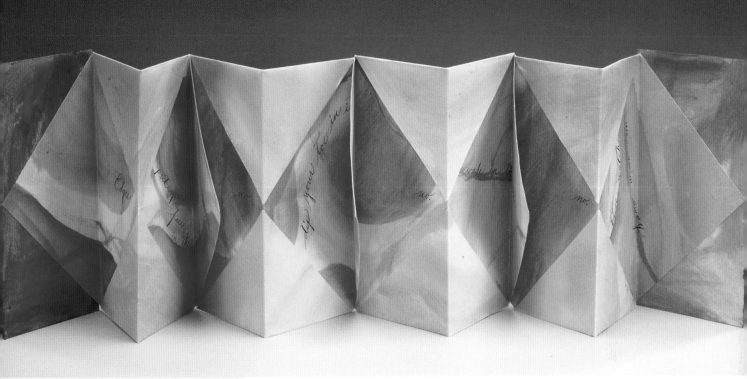

Tools: small paper cups or disposable container lids; spray bottle (optional); flat brush or wash brush; paper towels or clean sponge

Materials

Paper
One or more inks
(colors of your choice)

Example Colors

Indian yellow
Scarlet

Washes

Matisse had his assistants paint monochromatic washes over white paper so that he could have a stack of colored paper in the shades he desired for use in his collages. It's fun to make your own high-quality construction paper as he did, or use a wash as a background for future painting.

The term "wash" generally refers to a large area of one color. It can also refer to a blend of several colors applied in sequence while all of them are still wet: a graduated wash. Wetting the paper and the brush with water before applying color will give a more unified result. When multiple colors are used, a good blended wash shows one color gradually turning into another with no hard edges. The wetter the paper, the less you will see the brush strokes.

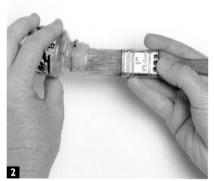

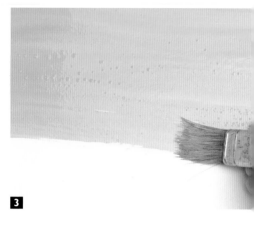

Note that too much water will leave an effect called a watermark, which looks like a sunburst or a cloud when dry. For a uniform colored paper, blot these puddles with a clean sponge or paper towel before they dry. On the other hand, the swirling color leaves an interesting effect, and you may want to keep it.

To prepare a wash you may spray the paper first with water. The photos in Steps 2 and 4 show different ways of applying undiluted ink; these are interchangeable.

For large areas, dilute the ink with water in a tiny paper cup or a container lid and dip the wet brush into this wash solution. Photos of this process are with the wet-on-wet technique on page 37. Try the proportions 1:5 of ink to water, starting with one dropperful of ink.

1. Wet the brush. You may want to use a spray bottle filled with water to mist the paper first.

2. Pour a bit of ink from the bottle onto the end of the brush or pour

the ink into a paper cup or a container lid and dip the wet brush into the ink.

3. Paint the paper in overlapping sections.

4. Add a second color by squeezing ink from the dropper onto the brush or by dipping the brush into another ink/water solution.

5. Continue painting, dipping the brush in water and adding ink or changing colors as you go.

CRITICAL OPALESCENCE, 2004; acrylic inks, letterpress, linoleum cuts; pamphlet stitch; edition of 40; 3" × 3" (7.6 cm × 7.6 cm), 4" × 4" (10.2 cm × 10.2 cm), 4" × 7" (10.2 cm × 17.8 cm). **Techniques:** acrylic ink wash, cut and pasted papers

***THANK YOU*, 2005;** acrylic inks, rubber stamps, hand-made postage stamps; single-flag accordion with envelopes; 5¾" × 4¼" (14.6 cm × 10.8 cm). **Techniques:** acrylic ink wash, acrylic inks applied with various brushes to hand-made postage stamps, rubber stamps

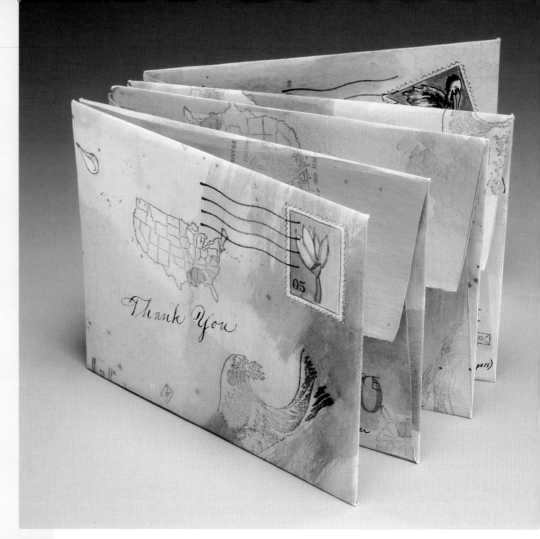

Tools: small paper cups or disposable container lids, spray bottle (optional); large round brush; paper towels or clean sponge; one or more rubber stamps

Materials

Paper
Pigmented stamp pad
One or more inks
(colors of your choice)

Example Colors

Black stamp pad
Light green ink
Turquoise ink

Washes and Rubber Stamps

To add dimension to your wash, try stamping an image on the paper first with pigmented black rubber-stamp ink. Pigments are more permanent than dyes, so make sure the stamp pad says "pigmented" and "lightfast." Most rubber stamps are small so that stamping with them makes a pattern that can still be identified, even when the paper is folded many times, such as for the origami envelope shown on

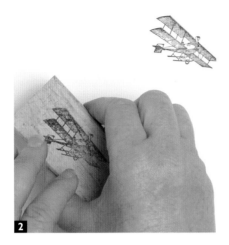

page 36 (top). They are a good scale for small books and cards. **Note:** the photographs show a large round brush; you may use a round brush, a wash brush, or a combination.

1. Press the stamp onto the inkpad. With a brand new inkpad, you may need to press on the stamp only once; an older pad may require several pressings.

2. Press the inked stamp onto the paper. Stamp many different images or more of the same one, inking the stamp each time. Let the images dry a few minutes. Meanwhile, clean the rubber stamp by rinsing it with water.

3. Wet the brush. Put a dropperful of ink on the tip. For large areas, dilute the ink with water in a paper cup or a container lid and dip the

wet brush into this wash solution. Try the proportions 1:5 of ink to water, starting with one dropperful of ink.

4. Paint the paper in sections, dipping the brush in water or wash solution as needed.

5. Add ink or change to another color as the brush becomes dry.

Techniques: acrylic ink wash, rubber stamps

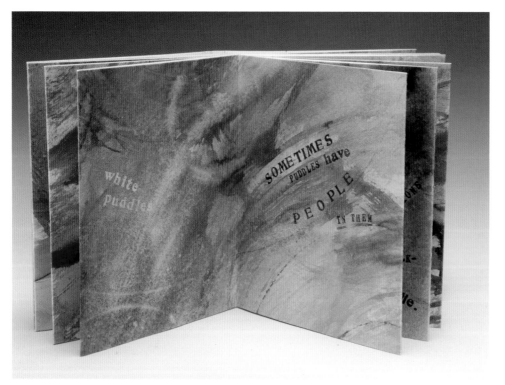

EARTH PUDDLES, **2005;**
acrylic inks, rubber stamps;
circle accordion; 5" × 6"
(12.7 cm × 15.2 cm).
Techniques: acrylic ink wash,
acrylic ink applied with
various brushes, rubber
stamps

Wet-on-Wet

Tools: small paper cups or disposable container lids, spray bottle; flat brush or wash brush; large round brush; paper towels or clean sponge

Materials

Paper
Two or more inks
(colors of your choice)

Example Colors

Turquoise
Light green
Olive green
Indian yellow

When you apply dots or lines of ink to a wet surface, the dots or lines expand. Try creating dots within dots or round nasturtium-leaf patterns.

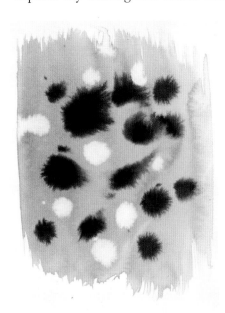

Wet-on-wet technique also works when undiluted ink is applied to the paper first and water is added to it. Apply a wet brush to one edge of a line of ink; the brush works like a wick and draws the color out into the newly dampened paper. This technique is like a graduated wash on a small scale and is a very effective way to tint the edges of book pages, to make sunset effects, and to shade objects.

1. Dilute one color of ink with water in a paper cup or a container lid. Try the proportions 1:5 of ink to water, starting with one dropperful of ink to make a wash solution.

2. Fill the spray bottle with water and mist the paper.

3. Dip the flat or wash brush into the wash solution.

4. Apply the wash solution evenly to the paper.

5. Dampen the round brush and dip it into a contrasting color of ink.

6. Apply circles or designs all over the paper.

7. Rinse the round brush and dip it into a second contrasting color of ink.

8. Apply the second contrasting color here and there or inside the designs you made previously.

9. Use a dropper and put a few drops of a fourth color here and there on the paper.

10. Gently blot up any puddles or shiny spots with a paper towel.

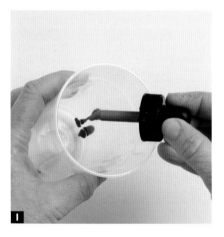

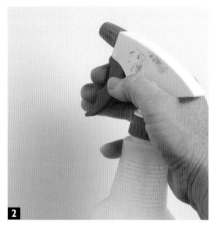

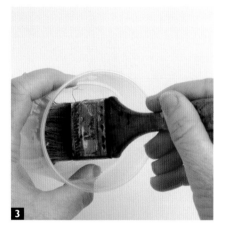

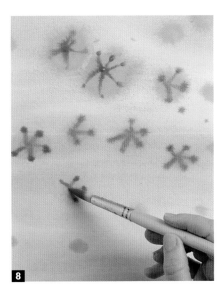

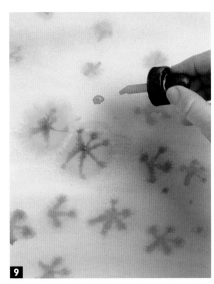

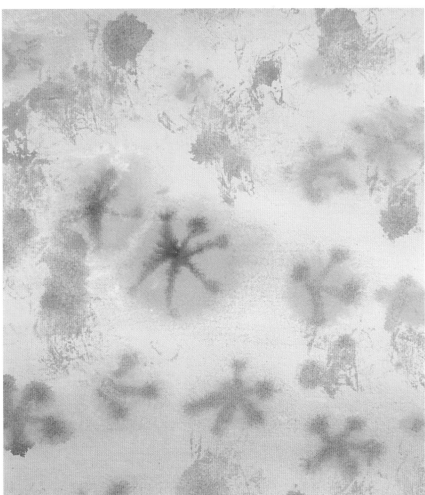

GENTLE EXPOSURE, 2006;
acrylic inks and watercolor
crayons; circle accordion
with black spine; 3¼" × 4¼"
(8.3 cm × 10.8 cm).
Techniques: dropper and
dry brush, watercolor
crayons

Tools: container of water; small
paper cup; large wash brush

Materials

Paper
One or more inks
Two or more watercolor
crayons
(colors of your choice)

Example Colors

Black ink
Red, yellow, orange, green,
turquoise, violet, pink
watercolor crayons

Washes and Watercolor Crayons

Watercolor crayons provide an easy
way to add recognizable patterns to
your painted paper. Experiment
with them to make repeating
patterns—look around and notice
that patterns are everywhere. Dip
the crayons in water and add
designs based on these patterns to
your dry paper. Draw lines, dots,
shapes, or a combination of all
three. Make several of the same

pattern in different colors, make different patterns, or write words across the page. Use another color crayon and write words over these words. If you like, dip a small wash brush in water and scrub over the crayoned colors, blending them together. Or try the following technique of drawing with the crayons into a wet painted paper.

1. Wet the brush. Put a dropperful of ink on the tip. Alternatively, pour a bit of ink on the end of the brush tip. Paint the paper in sections, dipping your brush in water and adding ink as needed.

2. Draw into the wet paper with a watercolor crayon, dipping the crayon in water if it feels too dry. Change to another color crayon whenever you like.

MARKMAKING EXPERIMENT

Once you have handled the tools and discovered the types of marks you like, try the following experiment. Or if you haven't handled the markmaking tools, just use a writing tool and make circles or scribbles wherever it is suggested that you make a design. The main thing is to keep going and not worry if the design doesn't seem to be what you thought it was going to be. The vision in your head is just a catalyst.

Take two pieces of paper of the same size. It doesn't matter what color, kind, or texture. You are using them for an exercise only. On one piece, make the same design over and over, trying to keep the design the same size. On the other piece, make the same design, but this time vary the size and orientation: rotate it, mirror it, make it large and small, let it run off the page, draw it quickly and slowly. If you used ink, let the papers dry. Now cut both pieces into quarters, eighths, or more if you used a very large paper. Look at the pieces side by side. Does one look more interesting than the other? Is one calmer? One livelier? Do they look different now that they are cut up?

The projects at the back of this book are made from painted papers that are cut into pieces in this manner. You will see that there is not one right way to paint paper. You will find that even papers you thought were unsightly change dramatically when cut into smaller pieces. Sometimes the ones that don't seem to work at all turn into the best pieces for bookmaking. Very small pieces can be used for a collage.

MAGNOLIA, **2005;** acrylic inks on paper; exposed stitching over paper strips. 5½" × 6" (14 cm × 15.2 cm).
Techniques: layered freehand forms, dropper, and dry brush

Dropper and Dry-Brush Outlines

Tools: eyedroppers (optional, if ink bottles don't have dropper tips); wash brush, large round brush; container of water

Materials
Paper
Line: dark
Fill 1: light
Fill 2: medium

Example Colors
Line: black
Fill 1: process magenta
Fill 2: olive green

Drawing with a dropper tip alone leaves a raised mark that, when left to dry, remains tacky to the touch. I accidentally came upon this technique when I used a dry brush to move around the concentrated lines of ink and was worried about the impending stickiness. When used with black ink, the result appears either like a crosshatched drawing or a black-and-white photocopy; it seems shaded and has depth. After letting the black ink dry, you can tint the rest of the page with a variety of colors. Transparent inks work particularly well on top of the black. The final product is reminiscent of stained glass.

1. Fill a dropper with ink by first squeezing the air out, then putting the dropper into the ink and releasing the bulb. Without squeezing the bulb, draw lines across the paper.

2. Brush across the ink with a dry wash brush. Wait about 20 seconds.

3. Dip a large round brush in water to dampen it, then add a contrasting color of ink to it with the dropper (or dip the brush into the ink).

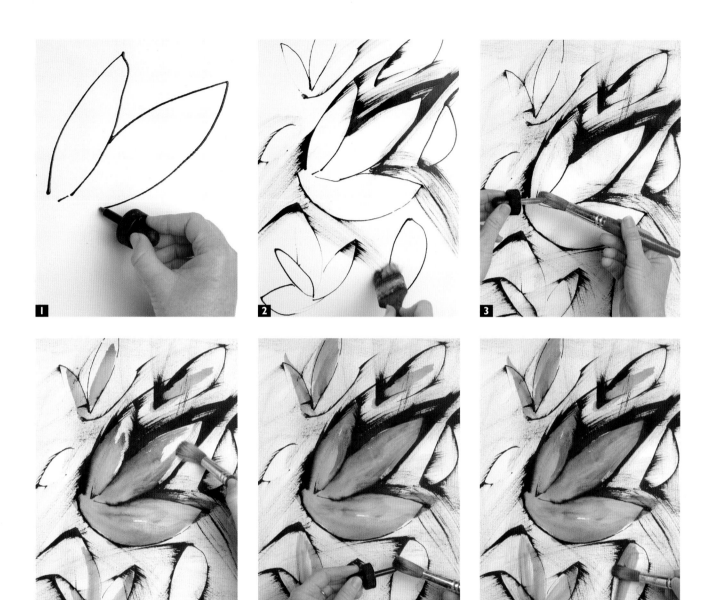

4. Fill some of the white areas with this contrasting color.

5. Rinse the round brush. Add another color ink to the tip of the brush with the dropper or dip the brush into the bottle.

6. Fill in some of the other details and most of the background or add this color in whatever amount you wish.

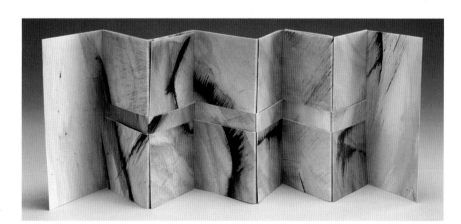

Technique: dropper and dry brush

Multicolored Droppers and Dry-Brush Effects

Tools: wash brush; eyedroppers (optional, if ink bottles don't have dropper tips); container of water

Materials

Paper
Three colors of ink
(colors of your choice)

Example Colors

Turquoise
Olive green
Purple lake

Technique: multicolored droppers and dry brush

In addition to the black-outline effect previously mentioned, you can create a sense of vibrancy and movement by using the dry brush over a variety of colors. For a spirited-looking paper, make marks with dropper tips filled with many different colors, brushing over each before adding the next.

1. Fill a dropper with ink by first squeezing the air out, then putting the dropper into the ink and releasing the bulb. Without squeezing the bulb, draw lines across the paper.

2. Brush across the ink with a dry wash brush. Save the dry brush for use with the next colors.

3. Add a second color of ink using another dropper, this time working from a different direction.

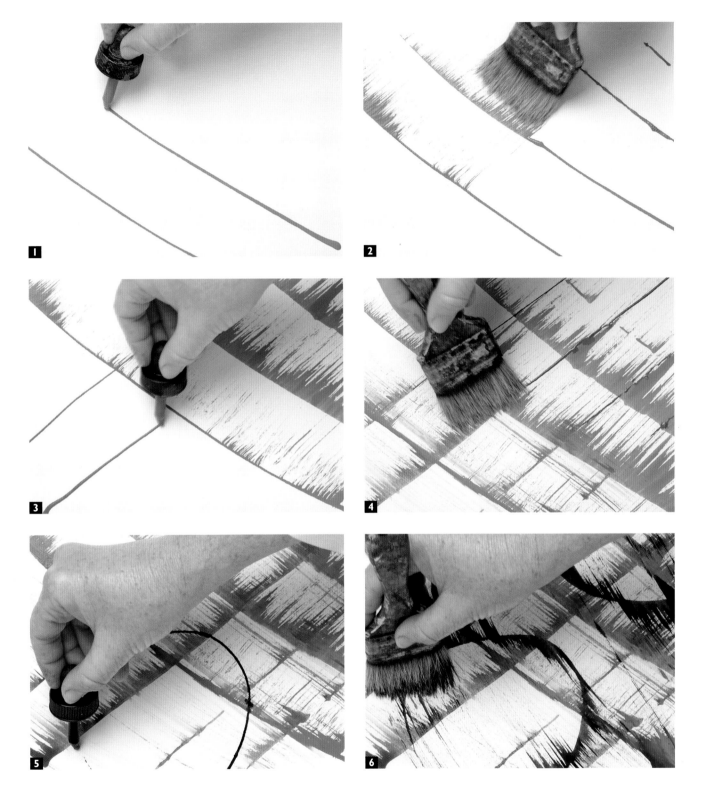

4. Brush across the second color with the dry wash brush.

5. Add a third color of ink using a third dropper. Make several large shapes, if you like.

6. Brush across the third color with the wash brush.

Brush-Handle Painting

Tools: small round brush; large round brush; container of water; paper towels

Materials

Paper
Line: dark or black ink
Fill 1: light or medium ink
Fill 2: light or medium ink
Background: light, medium, or dark ink

Example colors

Line: black
Fill 1: raw sienna
Fill 2: yellow ochre
Background: antelope brown

Holding the bristles and dipping the handle in ink may sound backward, but painting this way works very well, no matter what experience you may have. For this technique let go of any notion that you are in control of the line; the lines will become randomly thicker and thinner, leave blots, or stop completely, as if they were alive.

Drawing the outline of things, or contour drawing, looks particularly striking. I learned how to do this from Kitty Maryatt in a calligraphy class in high school. I like to fill the brush-handle painted outlines and the background with more color; you can do this by preparing a wash solution in a separate container (page 38). You can also add ink directly to the dry paper and then brush over it with a wet brush; this method leaves interesting marks.

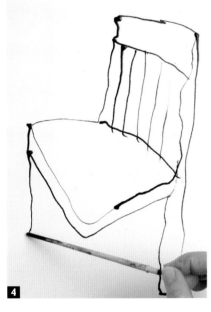

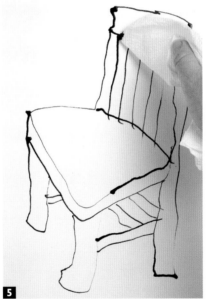

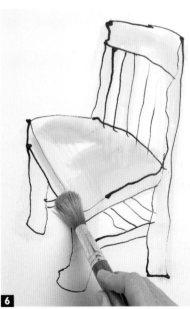

1. Dip the handle of the small round brush in the ink color chosen for the lines.

2. Hold the bristles loosely and drag the handle across the paper to make the outline of whatever subject you choose.

3. Continue dipping into the ink and drawing more shapes with the brush handle.

4. Add as much detail as you like.

5. Blot any pools of ink with the corner of a paper towel.

6. Dip the large round brush in water, then put a different color of ink on the tip of the brush. Fill in your outlined shape, or whatever area of your drawing you like. Repeat with another color of ink if you wish.

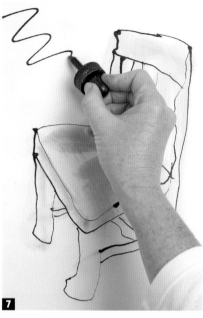

7. To prepare color for the background, use the ink-dropper tip or small or large round brush to apply one or more colors of ink directly to the paper.

8. Using a wet large round brush, mix into the ink just applied and spread it to fill in the background.

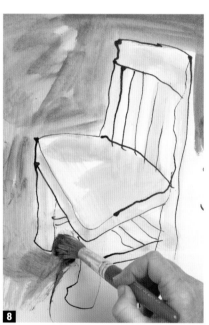

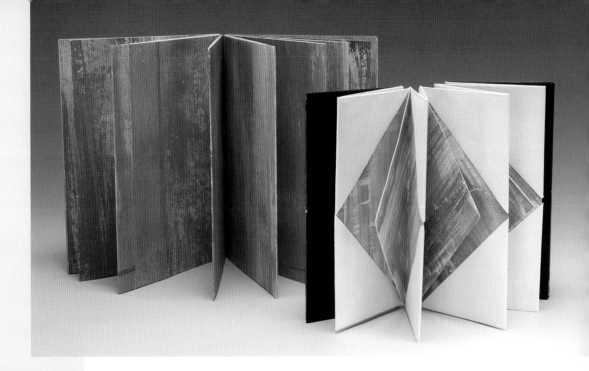

Techniques: (left) faux wood, Venetian red gesso and acrylic inks, (right) acrylic inks

Tools: small to medium wash brush; large wash brush; small round brush; large round brush; eyedroppers (optional, if ink bottles don't have dropper tips); container of water

Materials

Paper
Light: yellow or tan
Medium: red earth
Dark: dark browns or purple
Black: (optional)
White: (optional)
Pearlescent: copper, bronze, gold

Example colors

Light: yellow ochre
Dark: burnt umber
Black
Pearlescent: birdwing copper

Wood Grain

This pattern is loosely based on wood grain. It was inspired by a faux finish in Jocasta Innes's book *Paint Magic*. Try this technique twice, once using dry brushes as indicated here, and then again, using wet brushes instead.

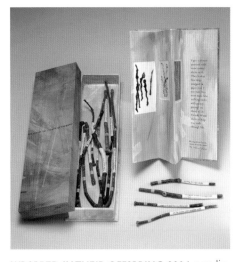

WRAPPED IN THEIR OFFSPRING, 2004; acrylic inks and gesso, letterpress, camphor sticks, linoleum cuts, accordion book, 3¼" x 10¼" in box 4" x 14".
Techniques: wood grain, gesso resist

1. Use a dry or slightly dampened small to medium wash brush. Paint parallel or wobbly lines with a medium or dark color of ink, letting the brush skip and leaving a little space between strokes. Wiggle the brush as you go, if you like. Rinse the brush.

2. Use the same wash brush and paint parallel lines with a light color of ink.

3. Use a small round brush here and there to add parallel lines or patches of a pearlescent color.

4. Quickly take a large dry wash brush and brush lightly over the drawn lines. Brushing back and

forth, perpendicular to the lines, gives a textured effect. Don't rinse the brush yet.

5. Use the dropper tip to draw other parallel lines with black or another dark color of ink.

6. Use the dry wash brush and brush back and forth across the drawn lines as you did in Step 4.

Technique: faux marble

Tools: one to three small round brushes (they can be the kind found in a child's watercolor set); wash brush; container of water; paper towels

Materials

Paper
Details (choose two): sepia, antelope brown, burnt umber, black, red earth, cool gray
Base (choose one): olive green, sap green, raw sienna, purple lake, red earth, silver moss, birdwing copper
Highlight: opaque white or another light color

Example Colors

Details: sepia, black
Base: purple lake
Highlight: beige

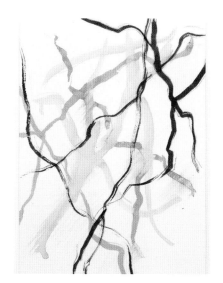

Marble

Layer neutral tones of acrylic inks to look like marble or use bright colors for an imaginative version of marble. Jocasta Innes shows an oil-based technique for faux finishes used for walls and furniture in her book *Paint Magic*. I modified her technique so it could be done with acrylic inks and paper.

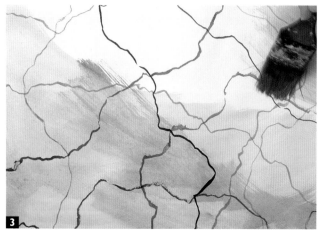

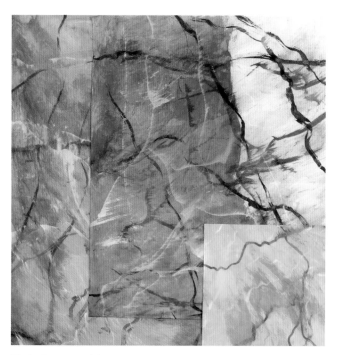

1. Start with one detail color and a small round brush. Dip the brush in the ink and draw a meandering line diagonally across your paper. Roll the end of the handle between your thumb and fingers as you paint to help you with the "meandering."

2. Rinse the brush and dip it into a second detail color to make more meandering lines.

3. Dip the wash brush in water and pour a little of your base color on the bristles. Spread the wet color over the lines you've already made. Make some areas lighter and some areas darker; don't try to give it an even coat overall. Let it dry.

4. To add highlights, take a small brush and dip it into a light color of ink. Make meandering lines again.

Variation: For a softer effect, use a dry wash brush and brush across all meandering lines from Steps 1, 2, and 4 before they dry.

Technique: marble

Technique: layered freehand forms

Tools: #16 or #20 large round or round mop brush or child's watercolor brush; small round sumi brush (such as gyokuran) or #8 to #10 small round brush or child's watercolor brush; container of water; wash brush or paper towels

Materials

Paper
Base: main color of ink
Fill: shade of the main color
Details: one or more contrasting colors or shades
Background: a different contrasting color
Spatters: one or two additional contrasting colors—white or a light or Pearlescent color

Example Colors

Base: lemon yellow for fruit, olive green for leaves
Fill: raw sienna for fruit
Detail: antelope brown for fruit, marine blue for leaves
Background: purple lake
Spatters: moon violet, mazuma gold

Layered Freehand Forms

An object can provide inspiration for a painted paper or become its subject. You can easily layer acrylic inks to indicate an object's volume or give depth to some elements. You don't have to paint the object realistically; you can add decorative gold splatters or paint imaginatively using unusual colors. Try working in a loose style, painting the object in

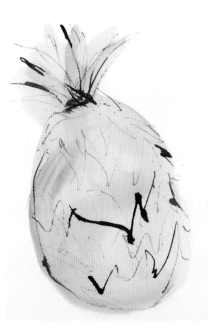

different sizes and shapes. Change the orientation so some forms are upside down or facing left or right. Overlap the objects to add more depth. Use different shades of the same color to add richness to the final appearance. Contrasting colors make the objects pop out; try complementary colors next to each other for a bold effect. The instructions and colors below apply to painting pineapples, but the technique will work for anything. Look around the room, pick an object, and begin.

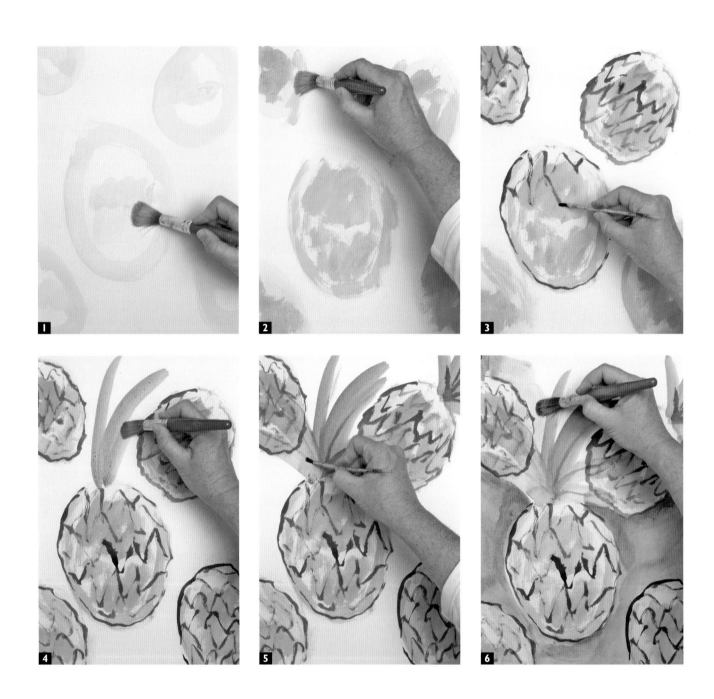

1. Block in a base color for the main portion of your object with the large round brush, leaving some white space. Rinse the brush.

2. With the large round brush add the fill color to any white space of the object or randomly layer the fill color on top of the object. Let the paper dry for a few minutes. You may want the ink in the next step to look crisp.

3. Use the sumi or small round brush to add fine details. If the ink bottle has a dropper tip, the tip may also be used to draw in the fine details.

4. Add other colors with the small or large round brush. This is the time to add another big element of your object, such as the pineapple leaves.

5. Add details to the newly painted elements with the small round brush.

6. Use the large round brush to begin to block in the background color. Try making the color darker near the object and lighter as it moves away by adding water as the color begins to dry on your brush.

7. Add spatters by dipping a small round brush into the ink, then holding the brush parallel to the paper and tapping the handle.

8. If you wish, add more spatters in a second color; be sure to rinse the brush first.

9. Take the dry wash brush and lightly and quickly brush any very shiny or raised spots of ink. The photo shows them being blotted with a paper towel instead.

Note: Spattering can produce large, raised spots; if these are left they will remain tacky, which may cause them to stick to other surfaces or leave ink marks. I recommend brushing them out or blotting them.

Technique: layered freehand forms

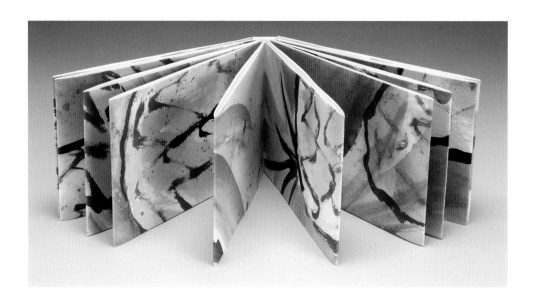

CENTURY, **2007;** acrylic inks, linen thread, book cloth, found objects; 8" × 5" × 1¾" (15.2 cm × 12.7 cm × 4.4 cm) box, 3" × 3" × 2½" (7.6 cm × 7.6 cm × 6.4 cm) book.
Techniques: wet-on-wet, layered freehand forms

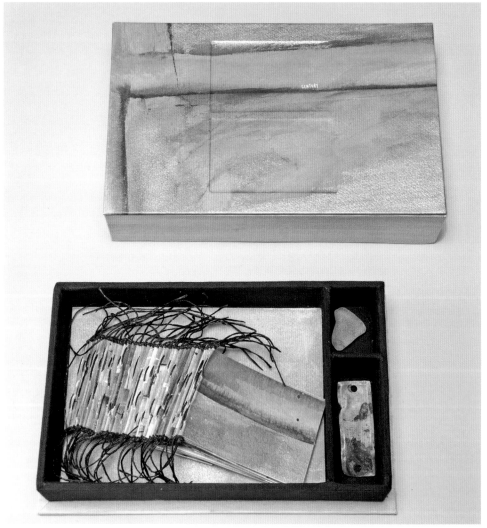

Techniques: acrylic ink wash over gesso resist, cards stenciled with acrylic ink and gesso

Technique: wet-on-wet

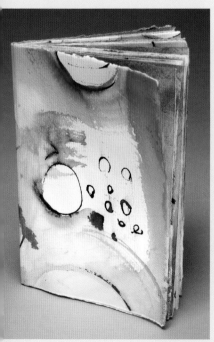

Patterning

Whenever we learn something new, we inevitably pattern, or model our behavior on someone or something else. We copy. We learn to talk this way. We learn to walk this way. We may learn to make art this way. Once we understand the concepts, we move on to improvising and inventing something new. It is understandable that you may want to copy one of the designs in this book. Realize that your marks will be your own because your hands are not the same as those of other people; you may hold the tools differently than others do; and you have ideas that are uniquely your own.

Patterns are about repetition. They are things we've seen before, whether they are actions or marks on paper. We look for patterns in wallpaper, wrapping paper, plants, music, and just about everything else.

Patterning is used often to decorate something to give it a pleasant appearance. In nature it serves as a disguise. As a disguise, a pattern fades into the background; as wallpaper it enhances a room; as wrapping paper, it excites anticipation.

After you find a markmaking tool you like, try making different designs until you find one that pleases you. Make it again. Copy your own design until you can make a pattern with it. This is the first way to decorate paper: creating a pattern all over it.

Once you've worked with patterns, you may want to vary your approach. For some projects you may want to modify the pattern, to add interest or surprise by rotating a shape, altering a color, or changing its size. The pattern can become more dynamic if you change something about it. It may also then cease to be a pattern, which is fine, too. Whether this newly designed paper remains the size you painted it, or you cut it into smaller sheets, each piece of paper will be unique.

WORD AS IMAGE

Handwriting is a form of patterning. In the early 1900s Gertrude Stein explored the use of word repetition as she wrote sequential sentences; each sentence varied only slightly from the next. She wanted the reader to be aware of multiple views of an

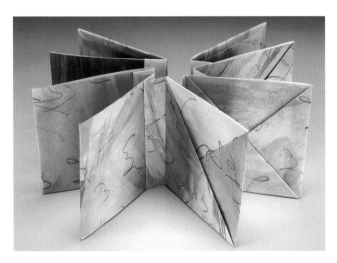

Techniques: acrylic ink wash, penciled handwriting under-layer

Techniques: layered freehand forms, white acrylic ink lettering applied with a ruling pen

WRITTEN, 2006 (open); cut sections of painted paper adhered to book pages

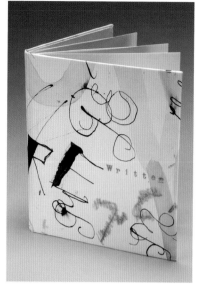

object or person all at once, patterning this idea after the layered paintings of Cézanne and the Cubist painting style of Picasso and Braque. The concept of Cubism was to try to show multiple views of an object—such as front, back, top, and bottom—in one flat surface, as if you could see all angles at the same moment. You can take word repetition, like Miss Stein's, and turn it back into painting. Even if you make a book where the words are cut up, the reader still has a sense of what the book is about; parts of words—beginnings, endings, solitary letters—will appear here and there, and in some places whole words will be readable.

Handwriting is also a form of style. A friend employed at a pen company often works in a booth at trade shows. Surrounded by a wide variety of pens, he encourages people to pick them up, but he says many people are reluctant to try them. If they hesitate to draw or scribble, he suggests they sign their names. Some do, but often they decline again, saying, "I don't like my handwriting." If you are one of those people who doesn't like her handwriting or even if you are one who does, the following exercise can give you an interesting look at your style.

You can incorporate writing with any of the painting techniques in this book; some of the photos can give you ideas of the results when combined with a wash, with faux marble, and around a painted object. Many of the markmaking tools (page 24) are good implements for writing with acrylic inks, or you may write with conventional writing tools such as a pointed pen, chisel-tip pen, or crow quill pen.

Put a large piece of paper, 18" × 24" (45.7 cm × 61 cm) or larger, on your work surface and assemble your writing tools and inks. Take any tool and dip it into the ink. Begin writing whatever comes into your head. Write one word or phrase over and over, or write about what you see in the room as you are looking around for something to write about. Change your tool periodically. It doesn't matter if the words are straight or if the size changes. The goal is to fill the paper with words

When you're done writing, cut the paper into eighths or smaller. The pages don't have to be exactly even, just similar sizes. Watch what happens to the words. Notice how your writing looks even better and becomes a visual pattern. Keep this in mind as you paint papers for future projects.

3 gesso & stencils

KNOTS, 2005; acrylic inks, acrylic paints, gesso, watercolor crayon; 22" × 30" (55.9 cm × 76.2 cm). **Techniques:** acrylic ink wash, watercolor crayon applied to wet paper, gesso, acrylic paint, sgraffito, dropper and dry brush

Gesso can be used by itself or in combination with acrylic inks or acrylic paints to add texture and pattern to painted paper. You can paint with it freehand or apply it through a stencil.

Gesso alone, when applied before any ink, becomes a resist: the acrylic inks do not adhere to it as darkly as they adhere to the paper. By taking advantage of gesso's quality as a resist you can achieve a subtle, damasklike appearance by stenciling with it first and then painting over it with an ink wash.

When it is painted on top of an already painted paper, gesso can add mystery and depth. Light applications or applications of watered-down gesso can provide a ghostly look, similar to painting with diluted ink. Thicker applications can be scratched into with a stick, skewer, or brush handle, in a technique called *sgraffito*, to reveal the colors under the gesso (see "Gesso and Sgraffito," page 67).

By using gesso with a stencil you can add texture and repeating patterns on top of or under the ink on a painted paper. You can add figures or create scenes, or tell a story with the stenciled images.

Gesso comes in white and a few colors. I used white to make the examples for the following techniques; try other colors for different effects. For best results, use stencil brushes (flat-bottomed cylindrical brushes) in a variety of small sizes.

See page 19 in Chapter 1 for a detailed look at gesso's properties.

***SHOULDER BLADES OF GRASS: BETWEEN THE EXPANDED PART*, 2006;** acrylic inks, gesso, watercolor crayon; multiple signatures with half cloth; 4¼" × 6¼" (10.8 cm × 15.9 cm).
Techniques: acrylic ink wash, watercolor crayon applied to wet paper, stencil with gesso, handmade stencil with black gesso

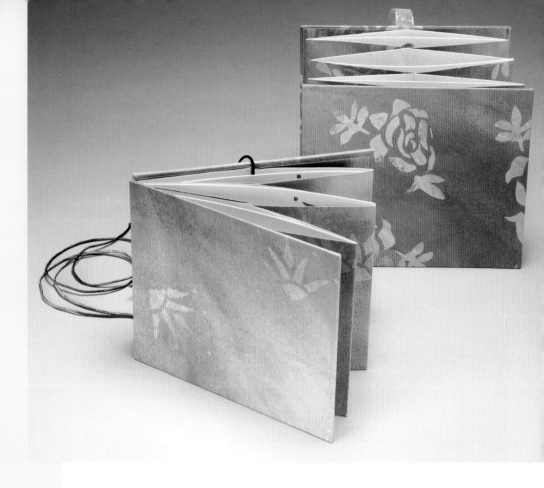

Technique: acrylic ink wash over stenciled gesso resist

Tools: large round brush or stencil brush; 3" (7.6 cm) wide flat or wash brush; paper towels or sponge

Materials

Paper

Gesso

Dark ink

(color of your choice)

Example Color

Purple lake ink

Gesso Resist

Add variation to an otherwise flat wash by painting parts of the surface with gesso before you paint the wash. The goal is not to cover the paper

completely with gesso but to vary the surface. Use an amount of gesso that is not so spare that you have to reload your brush every stroke but that is not so messy that it leaves globs.

Once the gesso has dried, paint over the entire paper with transparent inks or an ink wash. In the course of this painting, you will notice that the gessoed strokes or shapes seem to emerge from under

1 **2** **3**

the ink. The gesso resists the inks so that the final effect shows a variation in color, with the areas that were painted first with gesso being much lighter.

1. With the large round or stencil brush apply random strokes of gesso across the paper. At first, you may not be able to see the gesso on the white paper; that is okay. Let the gesso dry. Rinse the brush.

2. Add a dark wash on top of the gesso with the wash brush.

3. Continue to apply the dark wash while the paper is wet. If you don't see the white coming through, brush or blot the wash color; you may have used too much water or ink.

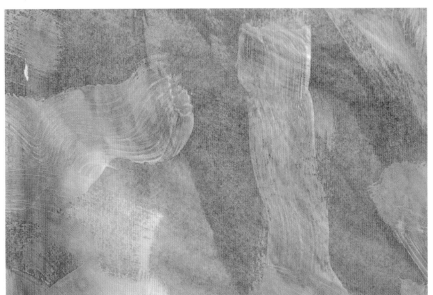

Variation: To decorate paper with a floral damask pattern, make a stencil of flowers and leaves and apply gesso through it onto the paper; reposition the stencil to create an allover pattern in gesso. Paint a monochromatic wash on top; the floral pattern will show through. The book examples in the photo show gesso resists that use mixed colors for the washes: one uses process magenta mixed with purple lake; the other uses antelope brown and genesis green.

Technique: gesso resist: granite

Tools: eyedroppers (optional, if ink bottles don't have dropper tips); 3" (7.6 cm) wide flat or wash brush; 1 or 2 small round brushes; container of water; paper towels

Materials

Paper
Gesso
White ink
Base: color ink of your choice
Spatter 1: black or silver ink
Spatter 2: gold or gold tone ink (ochre, raw sienna)

Example Colors

Gesso
White ink
Base: black
Spatter 1: black
Spatter 2: raw sienna

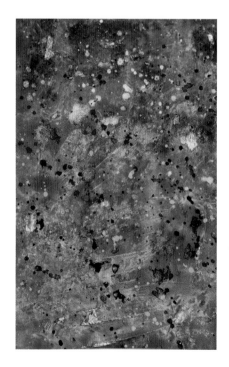

Granite

Using white gesso adds depth to this technique. The random brush-strokes of the gesso add a resist, which causes the wash color to vary in intensity. By giving the paper a natural appearance you can create a good base layer for the granitelike effect formed by the final spatters. Experiment with a diluted black as the base color in Step 4, or try a different color of your choice. A dark color gives the best results.

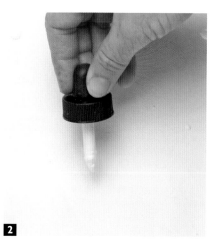

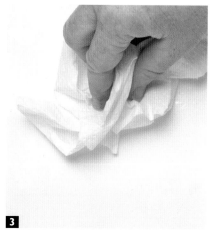

Preparing the Paper

1. Use any brush to put gesso here and there across the paper. The gesso may remain thick in some

places, but smooth out any lumps or ridges. Rinse the brush.

2. Using the dropper tip, release drops of white ink. Make random spots and splashes.

3. Blot any shiny spots or pooled areas with paper towel. Let dry.

Layering the Inks

4. Dip the wash brush into the water, then gently pour or squeeze a small amount of your base color ink onto the bristles.

5. Cover the gessoed paper with this tinted wash. Let dry.

6. For spatter 1, dip the small round brush in the black ink. Hold it horizontally, parallel to the paper, and use your other hand to tap the handle gently so that the black ink spatters onto the paper.

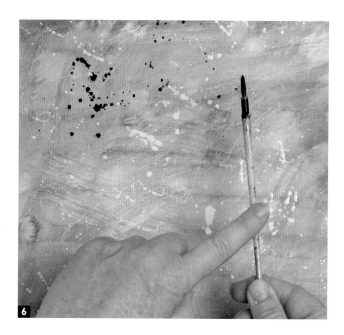

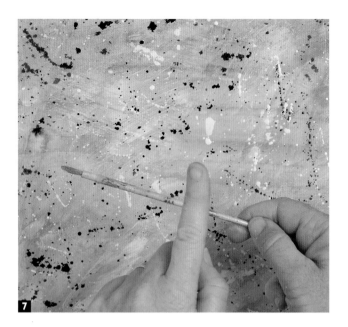

7. For spatter 2, use another small round brush (or rinse out the one used for the black ink) and repeat Step 6 with the raw sienna ink.

8. Blot any pooled ink or raised areas with paper towel. Let dry.

Variation: Different granitelike effects can be achieved when you work with various colors of ink for the wash and spatters.

Technique: gesso resist, granite

Techniques: acrylic inks applied with various brushes, multicolored droppers and dry brush, gesso, sgraffito

Tools: eyedroppers (optional, if ink bottles don't have dropper tips); variety of brushes (photos show large round and wash brushes); container of water; stick or skewer

Materials

Paper
Background: two or more ink colors of your choice
Detail: black ink
Gesso

Example Colors

Background: olive green, raw sienna, and red earth
Detail: black
Gesso

Gesso and Sgraffito

Strokes of fairly thick gesso on top of already painted paper add depth and a somewhat mysterious quality to the surface, especially if you scratch or scribble in it with a skewer before it dries. This scratching technique is called *sgraffito*. You may scratch whatever shapes you choose or draw lines that you can use later as guides for lettering; some of the color underneath will peek out from inside the scratches.

The following instructions describe the photographs, but you may paint the paper any way you like.

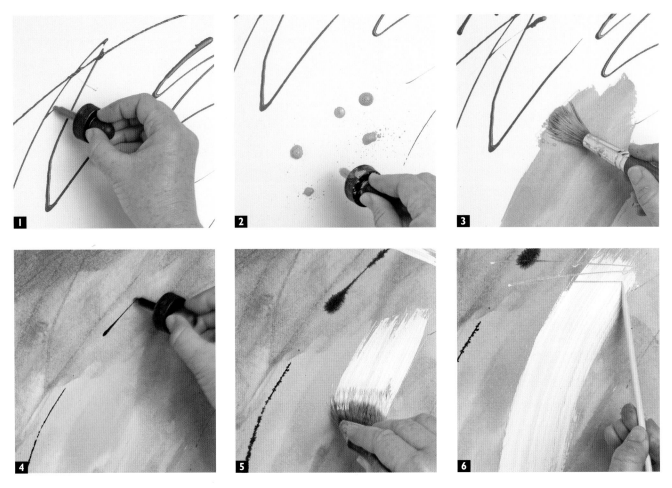

1. Using the dropper tip and one of your background inks, draw whatever you like on the paper.

2. Squeeze out spots of another background color with the dropper.

3. Begin blending the paint by using a large round brush that has been dampened. Draw on or drop on and blend in a third color if you wish.

4. Add more details with black ink and the dropper. Let dry.

5. Apply gesso in streaks across the painted paper.

6. Use the skewer or stick to scratch into the gesso. Let dry.

***GRAFFITI IN THE CITY*, 2005;** acrylic ink, acrylic paint, gesso; multiple signatures
with half cloth; 5⅜" × 6¼" (13.3 cm × 15.9 cm).
Techniques: acrylic inks applied with various brushes, watercolor crayon applied
to wet paper, gesso, sgraffito

Tools: letter stencils; ½" to 1" stencil brushes (1.3 cm to 2.5 cm) container of water; paper plate, or palette; paper towels

Materials

Paper

Gesso

Inks or paints

(colors of your choice)

Example Colors

Turquoise

Prussian blue

Basic Stenciling

Why use gesso to stencil paper? The stenciling medium needs to be somewhat stiff to obtain a clean, crisp edge: gesso is a good consistency for this. Acrylic inks are too wet to be used alone with stencils; the ink seeps under the stencil and leaves blotchy, uneven edges. Acrylic paint by itself, in tiny amounts, works well for stenciling; however, if you are making book pages, the acrylic paint on two facing pages may stick together, even when dry. You can use gesso by itself or mix it with the paint to give the paint a

toothier, or rougher, matte finish. Small amounts of ink may be mixed with the gesso to tint it, but you will need to make sure that your brand of gesso is very stiff to get satisfactory results when it is mixed with ink. Test by mixing half paint or ink with half gesso and see if the mixture is stiff enough so that it does not run under the stencil edge.

You will be able to control the paint better if you have a dry brush loaded with a minimal amount of color. Even if you use a thick medium the amount is crucial, because too much paint makes sloppy images. For this reason, always begin with a dry brush. The brush will become moist with paint, but don't add any extra water or your stenciled images will smear. If you want to change colors and have only one brush, rinse it thoroughly and dry it as much as possible with a paper towel. It is better if you have several brushes and can dedicate one to each color you wish to use.

Stencil brushes are distinctive because they are cylindrical and cut flat across the bottom. If you make a mark holding a stencil brush perpendicular to the paper it will be a solid circle. A trick to painting through a stencil is to choose a brush that is the proper size. If your images are small, use a small stencil brush. If your brush is too big, you run the risk of painting over the outside edges of the stencil. If your brush is too small, you must work harder and use more strokes. However, if you wish to achieve a pointillist look, with little, varied dots, use a small brush and change the colors from time to time.

The letter stencils used for this exercise are the plain cardboard variety available at most office-supply, hardware, and art-supply stores; they come in sets with sizes from 1" to 5" (2.5 cm to 12.7 cm). Letter stencils can be used to personalize your paper with words before or after you paint it. If you are making something that will ultimately be a gift, such as a baby book or wedding album, you might stencil names on the paper. If someone is moving, you might stencil his or her new address on the paper as a design element.

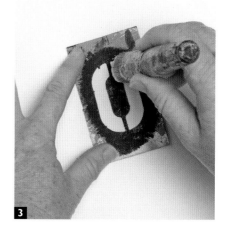

1. Put some gesso and acrylic paint or ink on the paper plate or palette.

2. Mix the gesso with the paint or ink. If you used the stencil brush for mixing, wipe off any excess gesso mixture, or find a dry spot on the plate and blot the brush there. If you are using a dry stencil brush, dip the brush into a tiny bit of the gesso mixture, just enough to color it. Twirl it around on a dry portion of the plate or on a paper towel so that the brush appears almost dry again.

3. Place the stencil on the paper. With an up-and-down motion like stamping, apply the gesso mixture through the stencil.

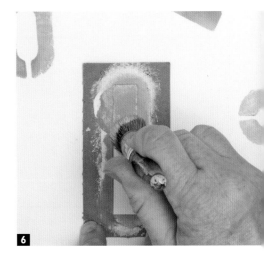

4. If the brush appears to have too much mixture, work from the center outward, moving the mixture toward the edges, continuing the stamping motion. Fill the open area of the stencil.

5. Remove the stencil immediately so it doesn't stick to the paper.

6. Repeat these steps to make multiple images from the same or a different stencil.

STENCIL-MAKING SUPPLIES

Have these materials on hand for creating your own stencils. They are listed in order of use.

PENCIL. Any kind. Sharp is best so you can measure and mark accurately. A thick mark will yield imprecise results.

TEXTWEIGHT PAPER. For making stencils for single-color images that you don't plan to use more than a few times.

DURALENE OR THICK FROSTED MYLAR DRAFTING FILM. For durable, easy-to-align translucent stencils for multicolor images (purchase from an art-supply store).

PERMANENT FINE-POINT BLACK MARKING PEN. For drawing easy-to-see lines on the Mylar. Sharpie is a readily available brand.

ART KNIFE AND SELF-HEALING CUTTING MAT. I prefer a #1 X-Acto knife with #11 blades. A sharp knife gives the best results, so keep spare blades on hand and change them often.

METAL RULER. To use as a guide for your knife when cutting straight lines.

PAPER CUTTER. Optional, but handy for cutting a set of same-size pieces of Mylar.

Techniques: acrylic ink wash over gesso resist, hand-cut stencil with acrylic ink and gesso mixture

Tools: pencil; art knife and cutting mat; paper plate or palette; ½" to 1" stencil brushes (1.3 cm to 2.5 cm); container of water; paper towels

Materials

Paper
Textweight paper or frosted
Mylar for the stencil
Gesso
Paints or inks
(colors of your choice)

Example Colors

Permanent dark violet paint
Raw sienna paint

Handmade Stencils

The precise, hard edge of a stenciled image makes a nice contrast to the brushstrokes, spatters, torn paper collages, and other curvy and organic-looking shapes. When you cut your own stencils you are in control of the

image—you choose the subject, you choose the size. No one else will have a stencil like yours. A benefit of handmade stencils is that you have the opportunity to try one out before you commit to using it in your project. Because you are using inexpensive materials, such as plain paper, you have the freedom to create many versions of an image from which to choose. You also can add details with multiple stencils. In the photograph of *Ladder* (p. 76) you can see four different stencils: one is the white figure, which is an underpainting (and became a resist); the second is the brown flame on the figure's chest; the third, the two ladder rails; and the fourth, the gold ladder steps.

When you are making a stencil, remember that the area you cut out will become the painted image. The negative space in the stencil is the positive space on the paper. To see the difference after cutting, stencil white on top of a dark paper (or as a resist and then paint over it), then use the same stencil to stencil dark on white.

To make cutting easier, turn the paper as you cut so that you are always working in the noon-to-three-o'clock position (if you are right-handed) or noon-to-nine-o'clock (if you are left-handed). This arc is where you will have the most control over your knife.

You may use one color or a mixture of colors within the same cutout. For this example, I kept purple paint, brown paint, and gesso all on one plate and alternated the colors whenever my brush seemed too dry to continue. You can achieve similar blends with any two colors. When you are stenciling, if you want the images close together, wait until one dries before you reposition the stencil. This will keep you from smudging the first image or picking up any wet paint on the back of the stencil and then transferring it to another spot on your paper-in-progress. The coloring medium will dry in a few minutes, but you can use a blow-dryer to speed the process if you wish (on low power, high heat).

Before you begin to paint, you might want to review "Basic Stenciling" on page 70.

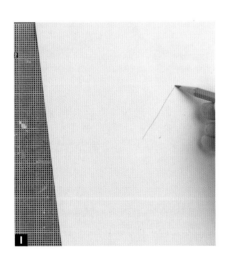

Cutting the Stencil

1. Leaving a margin of at least 2" (5.1 cm) around the edges, draw or trace the shape of the image you desire onto the stenciling material.

Place the drawing on the cutting mat.

2. Hold the knife as you would hold a pencil and begin to cut out the shape. If your design has

rounded edges or corners, turn the paper so that you continue to cut naturally. Hold or twist the knife loosely as you cut.

3. Remove the cut-out shape.

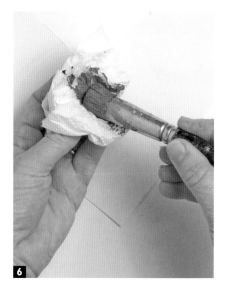

Applying the Color

4. Put some gesso and acrylic paint or ink on the paper plate or palette. (If you wish your image to be an uncolored resist, use the gesso only.)

5. Mix the gesso with the paint or ink.

6. If you used the stencil brush for mixing, wipe off any excess gesso mixture or find a dry spot on the plate and blot the brush there.

7. Place the stencil on the paper. If you are using a clean, dry stencil brush, dip the brush into a tiny bit of the gesso mixture, just enough to color it. Twirl it around on a dry portion of the plate or on a paper towel so that the brush appears almost dry again. With an up-and-down motion like stamping, apply the mixture through the stencil.

8. If the brush appears to have too much mixture, work from the center outward, moving the mixture toward the edges, continuing the stamping motion. Fill the open area of the stencil.

9. Remove the stencil immediately so that it doesn't stick to the paper. Let the image dry.

10. Repeat these steps to make multiple images from the same or a different stencil.

LADDER, **2003;** acrylic inks, gesso, stencil; multiple signatures over strips; 5" × 7" (12.7 cm × 17.8 cm). Techniques: acrylic inks applied with various brushes, hand-cut stencils with white, gold, and Venetian red gesso

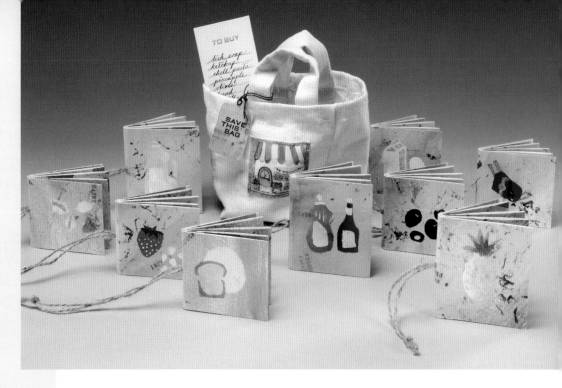

Tools: pencil; art knife and cutting mat; paper plate or palette; stencil brushes; container of water; paper towels

Materials

Paper

Frosted Mylar for stencils

Inks or paints

(colors of your choice)

Gesso

Example Colors

Mars yellow paint

Turquoise paint

Yellow ochre paint

Black paint

Multiple Stencils: Pochoir

Multicolor stenciling was used long ago on playing cards and Japanese prints. It was used extensively in France to hand-color fashion drawings in the early 1900s and is often associated with the Art Nouveau and Art Deco styles. The technique, known as *pochoir*, requires a separate stencil for each color. Those stencils were originally made of thin pieces of aluminum, zinc, or copper, and later of celluloid or plastic. Wonderful and refined examples of pochoir by Georges Barbier can be seen in special collections departments in some libraries.

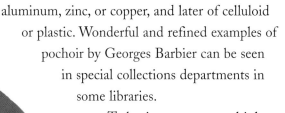

To begin your own multiple-stencil project you need a drawing or print of the image you want to stencil to use as a pattern, or key, for the stencils. It is easiest to work from a line drawing. Make sure that each differently colored area is self-contained, with a clear outline.

I use frosted Mylar for my stencils; translucent drafting vellum would work too. You could use transparent Mylar, but it blends in with whatever it's resting on, so I find it too easy to misplace. It is easier to see the image outlines on the Mylar if you draw them with a permanent fine-tip pen.

For this kind of stenciling, it's critical that the different colored areas align properly on the page so the completed image looks the way you intend; this alignment is called *registration*. An easy way to set up this registration is to make your key line drawing on a piece of paper the same size as the page you want to stencil (or draw the outline of the page size around your drawing), and then to make the stencils from Mylar cut to this same size. When you stencil, you simply align each piece of Mylar with the edges of your page. Also, because each stencil has the drawn outline of your entire design and is translucent, it's easy to align each in turn on top of the previously painted portion of the image. This process is explained in the steps that follow, and was used for *Night Monster* (page 83).

Before you begin, you might want to review "Basic Stenciling," page 70, and "Handmade Stencils," page 73. If you are stenciling your image more than once on your paper, begin by applying one color through the first stencil to all of the places where you want the entire image to be. Then stencil the second color in its aligned positions, and so on, going color-by-color rather than completing a full-color image and then going on to the next full-color image.

Cutting the Stencils

1. Make a drawing of your image on a piece of paper the size of the paper you plan to stencil. Make sure each area that is to be painted is fully enclosed. If you wish, you can color your drawing or use a number to identify the areas to be painted each color (#1 for the first color, #2 for the second, etc.). This line drawing is your key. Count the number of colors; for each color, cut a piece of frosted Mylar the same size as the paper with the key line drawing. If the color areas are small and not adjacent, one piece of Mylar can be used for two colors.

2. Align a piece of Mylar with the paper.

3. Trace your entire image onto this piece of Mylar. Mark one corner to identify it as the stencil for your first color—write the color name or the number ID. If you like, write that same number on all

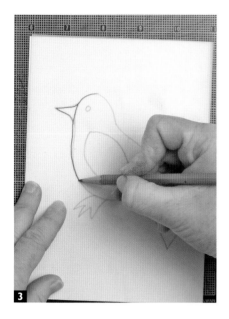

sections of the tracing that are to be painted that color; this way you'll know which sections to cut out later.

4. Remove the drawing. Continue in this way, tracing the entire image onto each piece of Mylar and identifying the color for which each is to be used.

5. Using the knife and the cutting mat, cut out all the areas that will be the same color in your first piece of Mylar. If another color area is contained within the first one, don't worry about it; you'll be making a separate stencil for it.

6. Remove the cutout shape (or shapes).

7. You will have a hole with a border around the edges. Set this stencil aside.

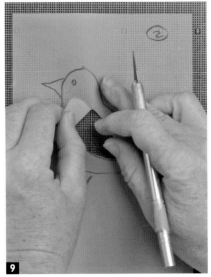

8. Cut out the area (or areas) for the second color from the second piece of Mylar.

9. Remove the cutout shape (or shapes).

10. Set this stencil aside with the first one.

11. Continue in this manner until all the stencils have been cut.

12. Note how two shapes that are not adjacent (the bird's beak and

feet) may be cut from one piece of Mylar. Since these shapes are far apart, they will work fine on one piece of Mylar.

13. The last stencil has one tiny dot cut out for the bird's eye.

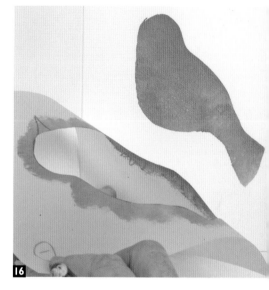

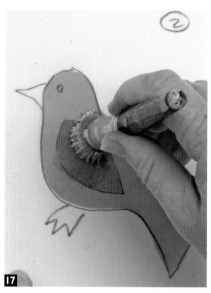

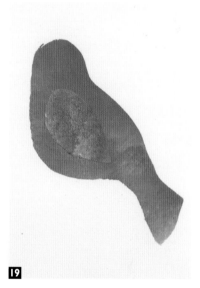

Applying the Colors

14. Make a palette of your acrylic paint colors with some gesso in the center. Make an acrylic/gesso mixture for each color.

15. Place the paper to be stenciled on your work surface. Align the first-color Mylar stencil on top of it. Apply the first color (see "Handmade Stencils" on page 75).

16. Remove the first stencil. Let the stenciled paper dry.

17. Align the second-color stencil and apply the second color.

18. Remove the stencil.

19. Let the painted paper dry.

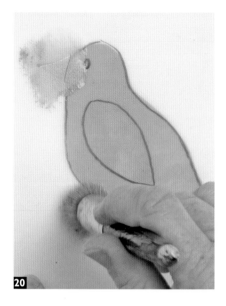

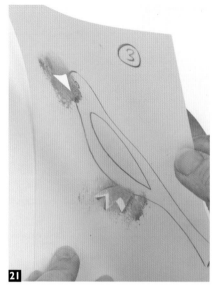

20. Align the third-color stencil and apply the third color.

21. Remove the stencil.

22. Let dry.

23. Align the fourth-color stencil and apply the fourth color.

24. If your design has additional stencils, continue in this manner until each has been painted.

He was often
CONFUSED.
He did not know
what to do.
Sometimes she
cried & he did not
know why. When
he asked she
would say it was
not him, but
what was it?
He could not help
so he picked up
his book & turned
pages, his eyes
staring, barely
following.

She woke up
STARTLED
but not scared.
She knew she had
been trying to shout.

Here he was wrapped
around her, warm—
soft hand on her arm.
She could feel his calm.

She knew they would
fall back to sleep again.
And they did.

If only she would always
have this dream.

***NIGHT MONSTER,* 2004;** acrylic inks and gesso stenciling, letterpress, bead and
waxed linen; 2¾" × 3¾" (7 cm × 9.5 cm).
Techniques: hand-cut multicolored stencils with acrylic ink and gesso mixture,
and gold gesso

4 *masking*

DRAWING OUT, **2005**; acrylic inks, acrylic paint, gesso, masked lines and borders; circle accordion; 5½" × 6" (14 cm × 15.2 cm). **Techniques:** acrylic inks applied with various brushes over artist's tape mask, stencil with acrylic paint, acrylic ink lettering applied with a crow quill pen

A mask is a temporary covering that protects an area while paint is applied. Once the painted paper is dry, the mask is removed to reveal whatever is under it. You might use a masking technique to preserve white space on your paper, or use it as wax is used in batik—to preserve a previously painted color as you paint over the paper again. The preserved space generally has a distinct edge that contrasts well with dynamic brushstrokes or can evoke stillness or order when juxtaposed with a quieter wash. Another aspect of the mask is that your shape need not remain white. You can tint the shape afterward in any color. If you use the pearlescent ink colors they will look like they are glowing where they cover the exposed shape. Even if you overlap this latest color onto a previously painted area, colors from the other areas will still show through.

For painted paper, a mask can be made with artist's masking tape or a film or liquid made for this purpose.

The tape makes it possible to paint to a hard edge without having a steady hand. It also leaves an inviting stripe to write on after it is removed. If the ink applied over the tape mask is particularly watery it may seep under the edges a bit, but this can be a desired effect, depending on the project. Masking film can be cut into shapes and makes it easy to preserve large or irregular areas. Brushstrokes of liquid mask leave a particularly mysterious-looking mark; the viewer wonders how one could paint with negative paint.

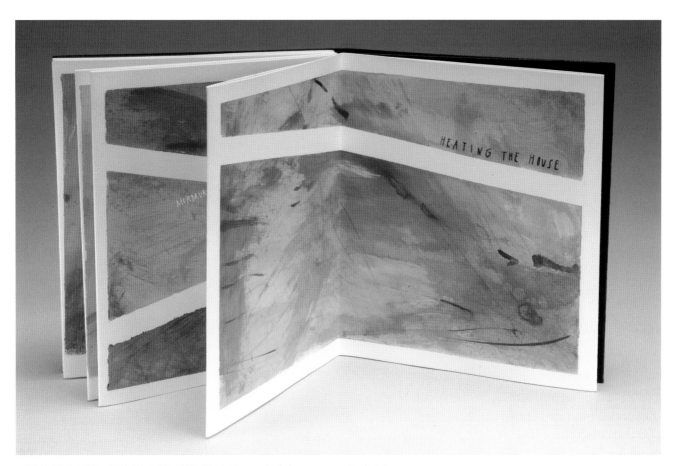

WARM MURMURS IN A HEATED HOUSE, **2006;** acrylic inks over masked stripes and borders; circle accordion, 5½" × 6" (14 cm × 15.2 cm).
Techniques: acrylic inks applied with various brushes, artist's tape mask

Techniques: acrylic ink wash, acrylic inks applied with various brushes, dropper and dry brush over artist's tape mask

Tools: eyedropper (optional), variety of brushes; container of water; artist's tape

Materials
Paper
Two or more inks

Example Colors
Black
Olive green
Purple lake

Artist's Tape

Use artist's tape for long, straight areas or for short squares. I don't recommend using regular masking tape; it will leave a residue on the paper, causing the paper to yellow over time. Check the different brands of artist's tape; not all are created equal. If you are concerned about the possibility of the tape pulling up a layer of the paper, choose one labeled

"low tack" or "for watercolor use" or "for paper" (not "for canvas"). If your paper is very smooth and crispy you may be able to use other kinds of artist's tape without mishap. Once the tape is removed, you can use your painted paper as it is or fold it into a get-well card or a birthday book and have people sign on the white stripes.

I used artist's tape to create the stripes in the books pictured above.

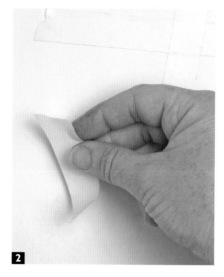

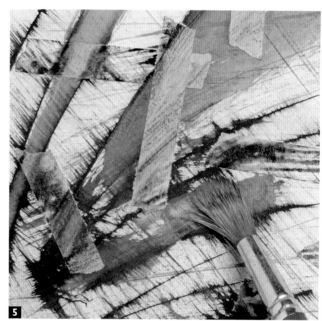

These books are examples of a book structure designed by Hedi Kyle that is known as the Crown Book. A detailed look at the structure and more information are in *The Penland Book of Handmade Books*.

1. Tear off small pieces of tape to create rectangular shapes or use long pieces for stripes.

2. Press the tape onto the paper you want to paint.

3. Use the dropper tip or eyedropper and dry brush (page 42) or another technique to apply ink to the paper.

4. Make sure to paint over the entire paper and over the tape as well.

5. Layer another color ink on top, using either a wash or a wet brush with undiluted ink or a combination of the two. (You may let the first color dry, if you like.)

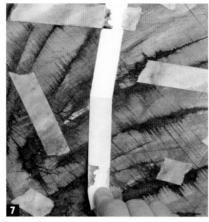

6. Add a third color, if you like. Let dry.

7. When the paper is completely dry, gently begin to remove the tape.

8. Make sure all the tape is completely removed.

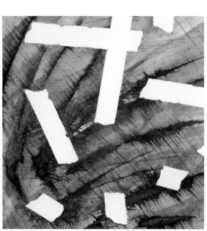

Techniques: dry brush and dropper over artist's tape mask

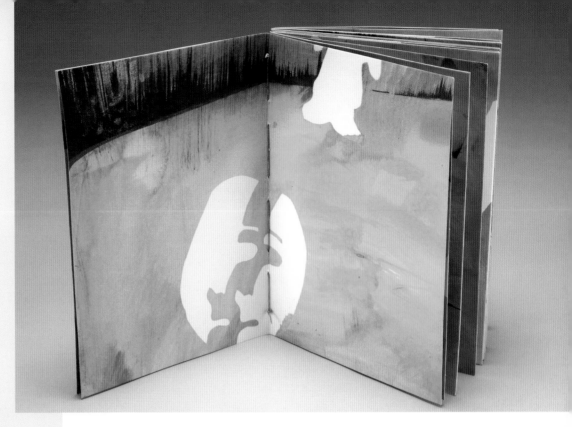

I WANT TO SPEAK TO
YOU IN YOUR OWN
LANGUAGE, 2006;
acrylic inks over
masking film; 5" x 7"
(12.7 cm x 17.8 cm).
Techniques: dry brush
and dropper over
masking film

Masking Film

Tools: large round or wash brush; container of water; masking film; Sharpie or other permanent pen; scissors or art knife and cutting mat

Materials

Paper
Two or more inks
(colors of your choice)

Example Colors

Indian yellow
Scarlet
Antelope brown
Black

Masking film can be cut to any shape and placed on the paper wherever you do not want paint to go. It is like a stencil in reverse; the cutout shapes become white instead of becoming painted. On the other hand, the film is similar to the stencil since both leave an unpainted area with a crisp

perimeter. You can find this self-adhesive film, often sold or referred to by its brand name, Frisket™, in art-supply stores with the watercolor supplies, airbrush supplies, or with other miscellaneous rolled materials. It comes in different widths; a smaller width—approximately one foot (30.5 cm) wide—is reasonably priced and appropriate for the projects included here. The film has a very low tack, which means it can be removed easily, and on most papers it does not leave a mark or residue or cause any damage. You might also experiment with low-tack shelf covering, found in many supermarkets and hardware stores.

Sometimes it is easier to work on a composition if you create some shapes first as masks, paint a background over them, and then fill in the masked areas afterward with ink. Say, for example, you want to paint a tree with many branches against a blue sky. You can cut the big shapes of the branches out of masking film first and apply them to the paper. You can then put a blue wash over the mask. After the blue wash is dry you can lift up the mask and fill in the details of the branches. It is much easier to do a quick blue wash than to paint the branches first and try to paint blue around each one individually.

Working with a mask can also make you feel freer—you're not taking a risk or making a commitment because you are not actually making a mark or applying paint. Cutting shapes out of masking film can be a good way to help you get started when you are feeling restless, blocked, or unsure what to do.

To get started, you might want to choose a photograph to work from. Select the major shapes in the photo, then make several sketches on paper of the shapes and pick only those you want to cut out. You don't have to use all the shapes in your picture just because you know they are there. As the artist you get to choose what goes in your picture. You can also rearrange, reverse, or change the scale of anything you wish. Then draw the shapes onto the film and cut them out.

1. Cut a freehand shape, as I did, or draw a shape directly on the clear film with a permanent pen. Cut out the shape, using scissors or art knife and cutting mat.

2. Peel off the backing and place the film on the paper you want to paint.

3. Paint a wash over the film with any kind of brush, being gentle with your brushstrokes: the film has a tendency to move if it is brushed too hard. I used a large round brush because I liked the kind of strokes it made, but a wash brush is certainly fine.

4. Draw dark lines across the film, extending them onto the surrounding paper to emphasize the shape.

5. Let the paper dry completely, then remove the film.

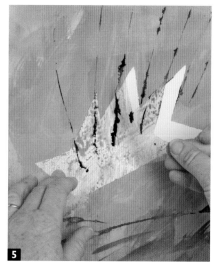

SCAR-CLOUD SKY, 2006; acrylic inks and gesso; 5½" × 7" (14 cm × 17.8 cm).

Techniques: dry brush and dropper; gesso over masking film

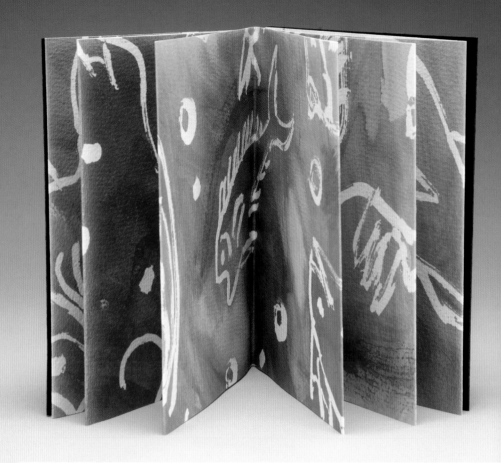

Techniques: acrylic ink wash over masking fluid (drawn with an Incredible Nib)

Tools: liquid mask; paper plate; masking nib (optional); inexpensive synthetic brush; fan brush (optional); paper stencils (optional); eyedropper (optional); paper towels; rubber cement pickup

Materials

Paper
One or more inks
(colors of your choice)

Example Colors

Turquoise
Scarlet
Process magenta

Liquid Mask

Liquid mask, sometimes known by one of its brand names, Frisket, may be used to mask small and large areas. With it you can create a freely painted line and also make more detailed images; you can apply it through

a stencil to create a crisp image. You can also write with it, something you cannot do with artist's tape or masking film. This mask is liquid rubber, usually in an ammonia base—if you have latex allergies, be sure to wear gloves and work in a well-ventilated space. The mask will destroy the bristles of your brush, so use a masking nib, which is made of an acrylic fiber that is much tougher than a brush and

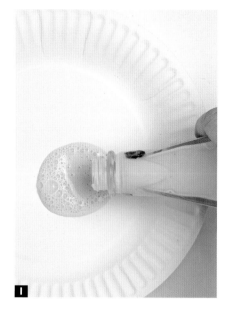

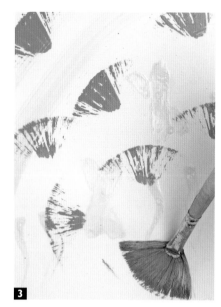

1. Pour some liquid mask onto a paper plate.

2. Using a synthetic brush, apply the mask to your paper through a stencil or draw thin lines with the masking nib or make a variety of brushstrokes on the paper. Let the mask dry completely.

3. Apply one color of ink with a fan brush, if you like. Let the ink dry.

4. Incorporate more colors by adding ink with the dropper tips or eyedroppers, or using washes, undiluted ink, or a combination. Paint the entire page for best results.

5. Blot any pools of water or ink with paper towel. Let the paper dry completely.

can withstand the masking fluid. Alternatively, use an inexpensive synthetic brush that you can dedicate to the mask and not worry if it gets messy. Rinse the nib or brush frequently and keep it as clean as you can.

Liquid mask must be dry before you paint over it. To remove it after

you paint and the paper is completely dry, gently rub over it using a rubber cement pickup, which looks like an eraser. As you touch it gently to the paper, the Frisket will stick to the pickup. Use liquid mask on watercolor paper or sturdy printmaking paper that can withstand a little rubbing.

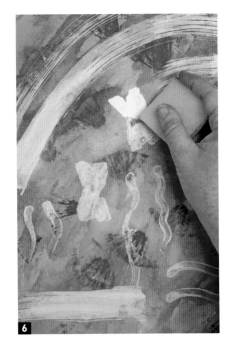

6. Using the rubber cement pickup, gently rub over the mask to remove it.

7. Peel up any large areas of mask with your fingers.

XOX, YIELD OR STOP, GATHERS, 2005 acrylic inks; Coptic binding; 5¼" × 6" (13.4 cm × 15.2 cm).
Techniques: dry brush and dropper over liquid mask

CURRENT UNDER LINES, 2006; layered acrylic inks over liquid mask, letterpress printed text, artist's carbon-paper drawings; woven codex; 4¼" × 6" (10.8 cm × 15.2 cm).
Techniques: layered acrylic inks over stenciled liquid mask

Tools: pencil; ruler; artist's tape
(low tack and/or it specifies that
it is for paper, not canvas);
variety of brushes; container of
water; paper stencils (optional);
paper towels

Materials

Paper
Inks (colors of your choice)

Example Colors

Black
Olive green
Marine blue
Antelope brown
Indian yellow
Raw sienna

Masked Borders

Someone once said to me, "I like the look of the painted paper in a book,
but I wish that each page had a frame around it." A frame makes a piece
look intentional, like a print or painting that is meant to be there, not just
an allover pattern or background. It confines our focus to one area of the
page at a time. One way to frame the decorated paper is to cut it into
pieces and glue the pieces to larger pieces of paper to create a border.
Another way is to use artist's tape to make a grid on the paper before you
paint it. When the painting is dry, lift off the tape to expose white borders
around many smaller paintings. In the example that follows, you can see
how the painted image changes as the borders are revealed. You might also
try masking fluid for a different effect, or use strips of masking film to
cover wider areas.

Use a large piece of heavyweight printmaking paper or 90- to 140-lb. watercolor paper for this experiment. Hot-press watercolor paper is extra smooth, cold-press has some texture, and rough is bumpy. Hot-press is easier to write on, should you decide to add text.

1. Measure the paper and mark it on all sides at the halfway points.

2. Measure and mark halfway between all the first marks and each corner. You will be dividing the paper into sixteen sections.

3. Center one end of the tape over one of the marks. Roll the tape out straight and center it across the opposite mark; cut the tape flush with the paper edge.

4. Repeat Step 3 for each remaining pair of opposite marks.

5. Put a length of tape along each outside edge.

6. Paint the entire surface of the paper using any techniques you like. Blot up any pools of water or ink with paper towel.

7. After most of the paper is painted, examine each interior rectangle to see if looks like a complete composition. Add stenciled images, if you like.

8. When the paint is completely dry, begin to peel up the tape. Work carefully to remove the top layer at each intersection first.

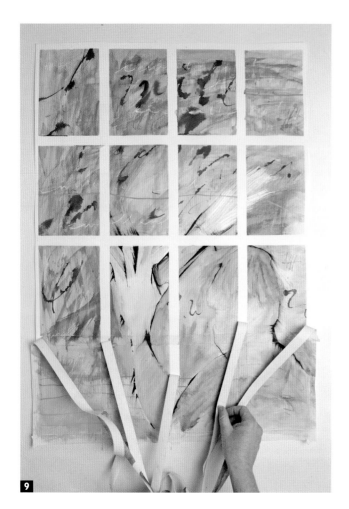

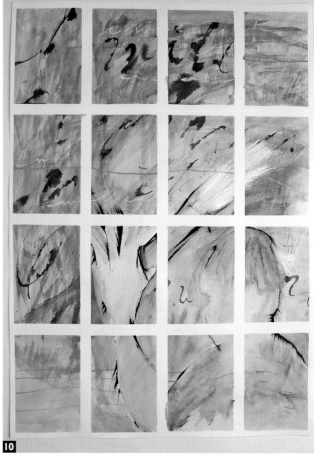

9. Continue to remove the tape.

10. When all the tape is removed, decide whether to cut the completed paper into separate cards or stand-alone paintings, or if you'd like to continue working on it to make a book.

Making a Book

11. Determine the grain of the paper (see page 122).

12. Make three parallel cuts through the borders that are perpendicular to the grain, separating the paper into four strips of four painted panels each.

13. Assemble as for a Venetian Blind (Steps 1a, 2a, 3a, and 6 to 16, pages 144 to 147). This photo shows one strip cut from the completed paper and folded accordion style, as when step 3a of the Venetian Blind is completed.

Note: if you want to make this into a Circle Accordion (page 122), read the directions there before masking and painting.

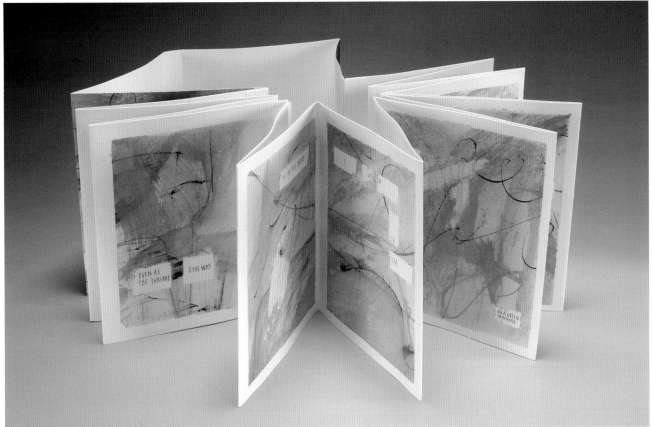

***AMENDS*, 2006;** acrylic inks, masked lines and borders, thread accents; circle accordion; 5½" × 6" (14 cm × 15.2 cm).
Techniques: layered acrylic inks, graphite, artist's tape mask, process magenta lettering applied with crow quill pen

5 paints & paste

A WITNESS TO CURIOUS SPEED, 2005; acrylic inks, Venetian red gesso, black and white gesso, paste papers, letterpress; three single-page folded books in triple slipcase; 3¾" x 5¾" (9.5 cm x 14.6 cm).

Techniques: wood grain, hand-cut owl stencil with Venetian red gesso, paste paper booklets with multicolored stencils in white, black, and gold gesso

One of the earliest forms of paper decoration was a technique in which paint and paste were mixed together, applied to the paper, and then inscribed or textured with a pattern. These "paste papers" were made and used as early as the sixteenth century, primarily as endpapers and covers for books. Artists today have adapted and varied the paste paper technique, usually using acrylic paints mixed with wheat paste, methylcellulose, or texture paste (molding paste or modeling paste). The resulting paste/paint mixtures give somewhat different effects, but they may be used interchangeably.

The addition of either wheat paste or methylcellulose mixed with water allows acrylic paint to stay wet much longer than usual, giving you the opportunity to apply it to the paper and then comb, draw, or add designs to it with texturing tools. Because it stays wet for a long time, you also have the opportunity to change your design before it sets just by brushing over it with a paintbrush, towel, or flat piece of board; you can start again easily. The paste does not alter the color of the paint, it just extends and dilutes it and makes it somewhat translucent. It also dries with a matte finish, meaning paste papers won't stick to each other. When this paper is dry it can be used for endpapers in a book, cover papers for books and boxes, or wrapping paper. For an interesting effect try painting with the paste/paint mixture over previously painted paper (make sure the paint is dry first) or on top of printed papers such as maps.

Both wheat paste and methylcellulose come in powder form that must be mixed with water. There are recipes for making these pastes on pages 102 and 103. Once mixed, the wheat paste has a very short shelf life, so mix it only when you plan to use it right away. There are three things to note about paste paint: The first is that it is too gooey to use with a stencil or mask. Second, once it is dry, you can work over it using undiluted ink or paint, watercolor crayons, or ink pencils. Third, you cannot successfully put a wash or any sort of diluted color over it.

When your paste paper is completely dry it can be sanded for a smooth finish and sealed with beeswax or varnished for extra protection. Methods for these processes may be found on page 116.

Use a vinyl tablecloth to protect your work surface, and wear latex gloves to protect your hands; the following methods are messy. You may also want to wear an apron or old clothes—once the pastes dry completely they are permanent.

If you want to pursue paint-and-paste techniques further, you can find many useful books. See the inspiring examples of paste papers and projects in one of Diane Maurer-Mathison's books. For other books about working solely with acrylic paints, try a book by Jenny Rodwell.

Paste Recipes

At least three kinds of dry powders can be mixed to produce paste for the paste paper techniques, or you may use ready-made texture (molding) paste. Each has advantages and disadvantages. Although it is slightly more expensive than the powders, molding paste is easy to use and will save you some time. Powder-based pastes are traditionally and commonly used for paste paper, most likely because they are readily available and inexpensive, but wheat paste, in particular, can be a bit lumpy. If archival properties are important to you and you want to keep your work acid-free, use distilled water; otherwise, you may use tap water.

All the pastes should be diluted to the same consistency. Your climate and weather conditions may determine how much water you need to add, but as a general rule, the paste should not resist your stirring spoon. The goal is to have a paste that is thin enough to spread easily—with large brushstrokes and no friction—and thick enough to hold the textural marks you make in it after spreading. Wheat paste should resemble a thick white sauce that will just hold its shape on a plate. Methylcellulose and diluted molding paste should be mixed to resemble soft hair gel.

When mixing the pastes with paint to use for paste paper, keep a spray bottle of water handy. If the consistency seems too thick, lightly spray the paste/paint mixture on the mixing plate and blend in the water. Repeat until the consistency seems right.

Techniques: variety of paste papers with sgraffito and handprints (left) acrylic ink wash, dry brush and dropper, rubber stamps (right)

COOKED WHEAT PASTE

Cooking your own paste is the least expensive method—all you need is all-purpose white flour and tap water. The paste will keep in a tightly covered container for a week or two if you refrigerate it immediately after use. Although this paste is the least expensive of the four mentioned here, it is also the least archival. It will work well for projects that are not meant to last more than a few years, and may be useful in a classroom setting or for gift wrap. I like to add some archival white glue (PVA), to help the paste last longer, because PVA already has some kind of preservative in it. The following is a recipe for a more archival paste.

Tools and Materials: white all-purpose flour; distilled water; two microwavable 1 quart (1 liter) containers; wire whisk; wire-mesh strainer; plastic mixing spoon; disposable 1 pint (¹/₂ liter) container with lid; PVA or preservative

Recipe

Use a ratio of one part flour to four parts water. For a useable batch, heat 2 cups (¹/₂ liter) water in a microwave on high for about three minutes. Put ¹/₂ cup (approximately 80 g) flour into a separate microwavable container. Pour a little heated water into the flour and

mix it with the wire whisk. Keep adding water a little at a time and whisking until you have a smooth consistency. Put the mixture back in the microwave for one minute. Whisk again. Repeat microwaving and whisking two more times. Don't let the paste dry up or overflow. Strain the paste into the pint container, pushing it through with the spoon, and then let it cool. Mix in about ¹/₄ cup (60 ml) PVA, if you wish.

Seal the container and refrigerate it. The paste should keep for up to two weeks. Mold will grow in this paste—as quickly as overnight—if it is kept in a warm environment.

COLD-WATER WHEAT PASTE

This is another inexpensive method, and more convenient than cooking your own paste. It will have the same properties as the cooked paste and should be refrigerated if you have any left over. I like the wheat paste powder from the mail order company Daniel Smith, Inc. If you are not especially concerned about archival qualities or how long your papers will last, you may use wallpaper paste instead of wheat paste powder, and tap water will be fine. You may mix a larger quantity than here, but one pint is a good amount to start with.

Tools and Materials: wheat paste powder; 2 cups (¹/₂ liter) distilled water in a small mixing bowl; wire whisk; wire-mesh strainer; plastic mixing spoon; disposable 1 pint (¹/₂ liter) container with lid

Recipe

Add 1 teaspoon (3 g) wheat paste powder to the distilled water and whisk together. If you add more than this you will get lumpy paste. Add more powder, a teaspoon at a time, until the paste is still pourable but not watery. After thirty minutes the mixture will thicken, the same way cooked oatmeal does, so mix it up runnier than you think you will need it. Strain the paste into the pint container, pushing it through with the spoon. Cover, let sit for about half an hour until thickened, and then refrigerate if not using immediately.

METHYLCELLULOSE

Methylcellulose isn't the sort of thing you can just pick up anywhere; you are most likely to find it in specialty art-supply stores that feature bookbinding or marbling supplies. It is easy to whip up. The advantages of methylcellulose are that it mixes smoothly with no lumps, and has a longer shelf life than wheat paste. The surface dries flat and not at all tacky. It is nontoxic and archival. Bugs don't eat it. Although its cost is three times that of wheat paste powder, you need only a tiny amount because it expands as it absorbs water. Be prepared to mix up this powder ahead of time, and let it sit overnight before you use it.

Tools and Materials: methylcellulose powder; 1 cup (240 ml) distilled water in a disposable 1 pint (½ liter) container with lid; plastic mixing spoon

Recipe

Add 1 teaspoon (3 g) of methylcellulose powder to the distilled water and stir. Add a second teaspoon (3 g). The mixture will still be runny. It takes about three to six hours before it begins to set. Let it sit overnight. Methylcellulose absorbs water and may become a gelatinous, foamy mass resembling tapioca or poi. Add more water and stir if it appears to have solidified. It should be about the consistency of hair gel, neither runny nor resisting your stirring spoon.

MOLDING PASTE

If you mix molding paste with acrylic paint and add water, it is terrific for making paste papers. It is the easiest paint/paste mixture to use, but it is also the

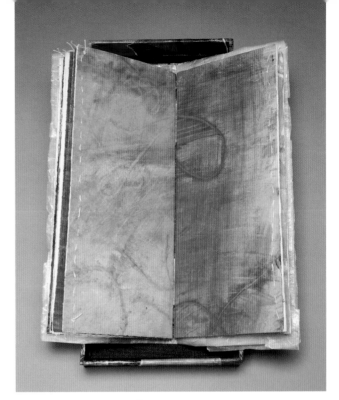

Technique: paste paper frottage

most costly. The convenience may be worth the expense, especially if your time is limited. You don't have to cook or mix it ahead or wait for it to set up at the right consistency, and it dries more quickly than wheat paste or methylcellulose. You can see it being used in the photos for "Paste Paper," page 104.

Tools and Materials: plastic spoon or large, flat, wooden craft stick; mixing plate (paper is fine); acrylic paint; water; spray bottle (optional)

Recipe

Place ¼ cup (60 ml) molding paste on a mixing plate. Mix in ½ teaspoon (5 ml) acrylic paint. Mix in water, 1 tablespoon (1.5 ml) at a time, until the consistency is workable. It should look and feel like pudding, and you should be able to spread it in large strokes. You can spray the mixture on your plate with water and stir instead of measuring out tablespoons. Double or triple the quantity if you are painting more than one large sheet (such as 25" × 37" or 63.5 cm × 94 cm) of paper, or make several colors at once.

Tools: paper plate; large wash brushes; spray bottle filled with water; sponge; texturing tools

Materials

Textweight paper
Wheat paste, methylcellulose, or modeling paste, mixed as directed (pages 102 to 103)
Acrylic paints
(colors of your choice)

Example Colors

Turquoise
Yellow oxide

Paste Paper

Use a paint/paste mixture to paint directly onto a piece of plain paper, or consider painting on top of previously painted or printed papers, such as maps, to add interest and layered depth to your work. Illuminated paintings and manuscripts often have shiny gold as an underlayer, which makes them appear to be glowing or illuminated from below. To achieve an illuminated effect, paint the paper with gold gesso first, let it dry, and then apply the paint/paste mixture over it.

You can use all sorts of implements to add texture to the paint/paste mixture on your paper. Try texturing tools from a hardware store, hair combs, old credit cards cut with notches, a paintbrush handle, or a skewer.

Because the paste doesn't alter the paint color, there is no exact rule for proportioning paste to paint. The technique that follows is a suggested starting point; feel free to explore and experiment—whatever you do will yield something interesting.

Be aware that paper takes a long time to dry, so make sure you have a place to hang it or to lay it flat (see "Drying Wet Paper," page 12). Now, mix up one of the pastes discussed in this chapter and continue as directed below.

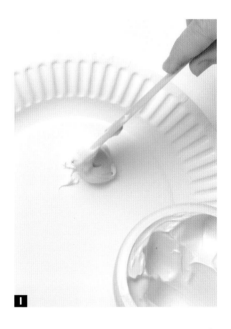  

1. Place ½ to 1 cup (120 ml to 235 ml) prepared paste onto a portion of the plate.

2. Add 1 to 2 teaspoons (5 ml to 10 ml) of each color of acrylic paint you want to use to the plate.

3. Mix the paste into the individual colors, dividing it between them. Use one large wash brush per color. You may mix more paint/paste colors this way at this time, if you wish.

4. Mist the paper with water from the spray bottle.

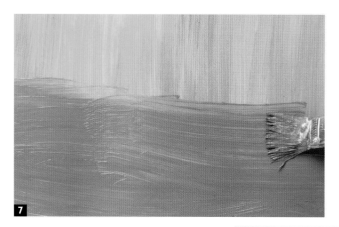

5. Dampen the sponge and wipe the paper with it.

6. Spread one color mixture on the paper.

7. Paint a second color over the top or add stripes or patches if you like.

8. Use your chosen texturing implements to draw in the paste/paint. You could also make handprints, if you like.

Tools: flat objects, such as paper stencils, tags, pieces of torn paper, tickets, etc; paper plate or small containers; large wash brushes; spray bottle filled with water; sponge; plastic card (an old credit card is fine); paper towels

Materials

Textweight paper
Wheat paste, methylcellulose, or modeling paste, mixed as directed (pages 102 to 103)
Color 1: light
Color 2: medium
Color 3: dark

Example Colors

Yellow oxide
Red oxide
Cobalt blue

Paste Paper Frottage

This is a variation of the basic paste paper method. With this technique you will remove much of the paste and paint combination, revealing a texture. In one class I taught, student and colleague Alice Armstrong said she didn't want to get my stencils dirty, so she put them under the paper instead, revealing this technique, which is something between scraping

and rubbing. *Sgraffito* is the technical painting term for scraping. *Frottage* is another name for rubbing. Other technical terms may be found in a wonderful encyclopedic book by Hazel Harrison.

Normally we think of this kind of rubbing being done with a drawing implement, such as a pencil or the side of a crayon, on top of paper that is placed over something textured, such as the sidewalk or the letters or pictures on a memorial plaque. For this paste paper technique you put flat, textured objects under the painted paper, then scrape off some of the paint with the edge of a piece of board or an old plastic credit card.

See "Paste Paper," page 103, for directions on mixing the paint and paste together.

1. Arrange the flat objects on your work surface.

2. Put a piece of paper over the objects.

3. If you haven't already done so, mix acrylic paint with paste, using one plate or container and one brush for each color.

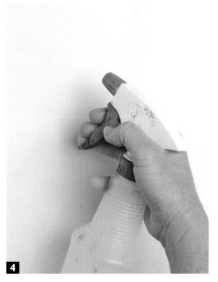

4. Mist the paper with water from the spray bottle.

5. Dampen the sponge and wipe the paper with it.

6. Paint the paper with the light color of paste/paint mixture.

7. Use the second, medium, color mixture as an accent.

8. Use the third, dark, color mixture to add depth.

9. Use the edge of a plastic card to scrape over the surface of the paper. Make sure there are no thick areas of paste/paint. You'll begin to see the outlines of the objects underneath.

 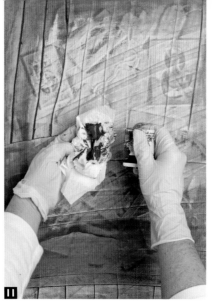 

10. Scrape in another direction, moving the mixture out to the edges of the paper.

11. Wipe the card when it becomes too full of the paint mixture.

12. Take some of the dark paint and scrape it back into the hollowed-out areas to help define the edges of the objects underneath. If your paper is large, lift it up and move the objects around; replace the paper and continue to scrape away the paste/paint.

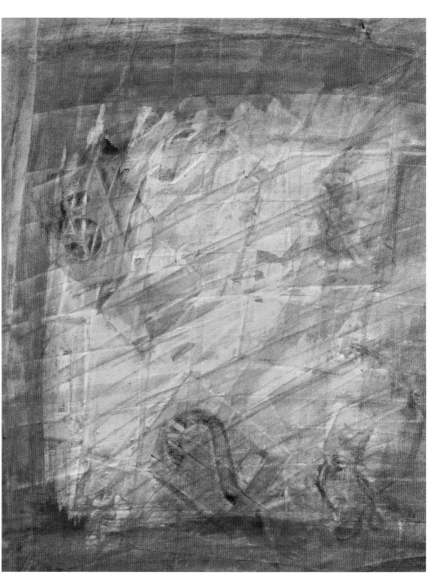

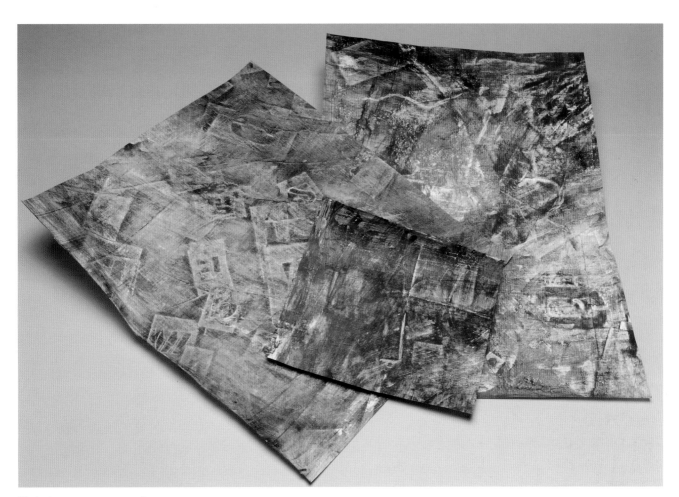

Technique: paste paper frottage

BARGAIN BOOK BIN, 2007; acrylic inks, acrylic paints and paste, collage, mirror;
8" × 8" × 8½" (20.3 cm × 20.3 cm × 21.6 cm) bin, 3⅜" × 5¼" (8.6 cm × 13.3 cm) books.
Techniques: drawing with dropper, layered color, paste paper frottage, collage

FORTUNE-TELLING CHIPS, 2005; assortment of pasted and painted papers collaged over small pieces of museum board housed in a pre-made metal canister.

Techniques: paste papers, acrylic ink–painted papers, collage

Tools: spray bottle filled with water; sponge; paper plates or small containers; large wash brushes; stick or skewer

Materials

Paper

Wheat paste, methylcellulose, or modeling paste, mixed as directed (pages 102 to 103)

Acrylic paints (colors of your choice)

Paper strips with printed or handwritten words, cut in small segments

Example Colors

Dioxazine purple

Cobalt blue

Collage

Before paste paper dries, you have a chance to add layers of torn or cut papers to it. Here's a big, sticky piece of paper. What will you put on it? Arranging and sticking other bits to a support paper to form patterns or a

new composition is known as *collage.* The word derives from the French verb *coller,* meaning to stick, paste, or glue. Since we are using pastes in this chapter it seems natural to think of pasting papers to make some kind of collage.

You can arrange painted paper scraps, bus transfers, tickets, maps, or any other lightweight paper bits and stick them to the paste paper support. Because the paste takes a long time to dry, you have plenty of time to experiment with collage effects.

For an integrated look, try brushing across the edges of the paper bits with your paste/paint brush so they blend with the background. When the paste paper is wet it doesn't appear very sticky, but as it dries it will hold the added paper bits in place. You can also seal the collage by brushing clear paste or the paste/paint mixture over the completed paper while it is wet or by using one of the finish techniques (page 116) after it dries.

In the woven accordion books on page 116, strips of glassine paper with typewritten words on them were collaged onto the paste paper support. If you want to use words in your collage, a customized way to do this is to type and print your own. For example, you might choose a theme and think of words that relate to it, then type the words, each on a separate line, double-spaced. Print them on cotton résumé paper or use a typewriter and type them directly onto any textweight paper, then cut them apart.

If your base paper is lightweight and you will be using it to wrap boards for books, attach only lightweight papers. Lightweight papers will buckle if the weight of the attached papers is too heavy. If you want to use thicker pieces for your collage, such as tags or cutouts from postcards, start with a heavier or thicker paper. You can use the thicker paper for cards or some of the pages of the accordion-fold books.

See "Paste Paper," page 104 for directions on mixing the paint and paste together.

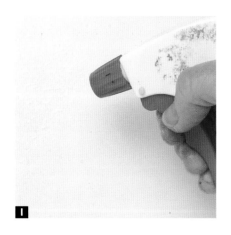  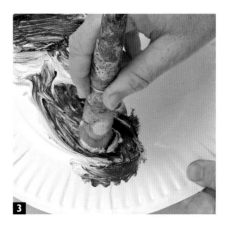

1. Mist the paper with water from the spray bottle.

2. Dampen the sponge and wipe the paper with it.

3. Mix individual acrylic paints with the paste. You may want to reserve some clear paste for sealing the collage.

4. Apply the mixtures to the paper.

5. Completely cover the paper with the mixtures.

6. Use the stick or skewer to draw into the paste/paint, if you like.

7. Put word bits here and there on the wet paste/paint.

8. Apply some of the reserved clear paste or the paste/paint mixture itself over the word bits to ensure they will stick completely and be protected.

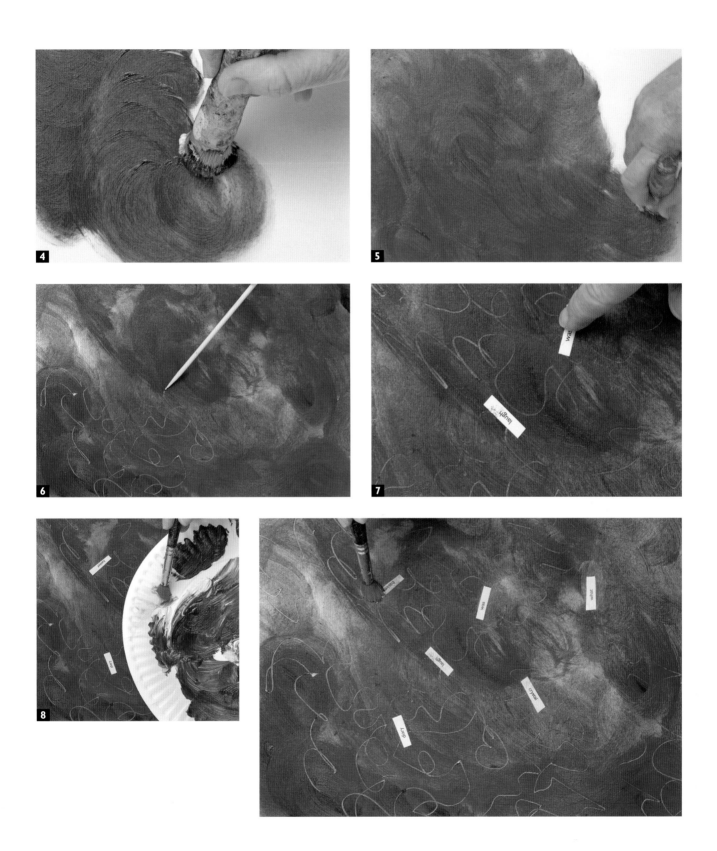

Techniques: paste papers, collaged bits of glassine paper with typed words

Surface Finishes for Painted Paper

While almost all the painting techniques in this book are completed as soon as they are dry, you may further enhance or protect the painted papers by choosing from a few different options. You may find that you'd like a smoother surface for your paste papers. If so, you can simply sand them. Acrylic colors are permanent and don't require a protective finish, but you might want to add one to projects that you would like especially to preserve or if your paper will be handled frequently. Beeswax will seal the painting without altering its appearance. On the other hand, if you'd like a glossy finish, you can coat the paper with acrylic varnish. You may also use varnish to protect and strengthen papers or boards used for book covers or boxes.

SANDED FINISH

If you'd like to smooth the surface of paste paper or a book cover that's textured with straight molding paste, sand it. Begin with a medium-grit sandpaper, wrapping it around a block of wood or soup can and then rubbing it gently over the paper. Change to a finer grit and repeat. Brush off any debris with a large wash brush.

WAXED FINISH

Beeswax is the best option when you want to give a protective coating to your finished paper without altering the way it looks You may use it on paste papers to protect them or on gesso-painted papers to make the gesso feel smooth and more pleasant to the touch. It makes a good seal for watercolor crayons and graphite. You can usually find a small cake of beeswax at a store that sells bookbinding or sewing supplies, or

A cake of beeswax being rubbed over a stenciled paper.

look for it online under "solid beeswax." Simply rub the cake of wax gently over the paper and then buff the paper with a soft cotton cloth.

Beeswax or carnauba (also spelled carnuba) polishes and other furniture polishes will also work; I can't guarantee their archivability and I won't use them in bookmaking unless I know what else they contain. They are perfectly suitable for cards and gift wrap, however. If you use one of these sprays, mists, or polishes, use it sparingly and buff the paper afterward. It may add a slight sheen.

VARNISH

Acrylic varnish will add a high gloss to your painted paper and provide extra protection to the painted covers of a book. It also will protect watercolor crayons and graphite so they won't smudge or smear. You can also use it to make certain areas of the painted paper extra shiny. It is sold in art-supply stores with gel medium, molding paste, and other acrylic media. You might want to buy a very small bottle of it at first, then, if you like it, you can buy more in a larger size.

A soft brush, such as a foam brush, works best for applying the varnish, but you can use any of your brushes; just be sure to rinse them with water immediately after use. To use the varnish, dip the brush in it and apply a thin, even coat to the paper. You can also use a cotton swab just to highlight or protect very small areas. Let it dry completely before handling it, or your fingerprints will be added to your project as a permanent feature.

GEL MEDIUM

In the paste section we discussed using texture paste (molding paste) for paste papers, but the molding paste, which is a kind of gel medium, can also be used as a finish. It is slightly milky and dries to a translucent finish (you can see through it, but it isn't crystal clear). You can use the medium straight from the jar and smooth it onto decorated papers or book covers. Add texture by drawing into it, molding it, or building up three-dimensional layers with other papers or objects, if you like. You can also mix the molding paste with acrylic paint beforehand, or paint over it with acrylic paint afterward. Experiment with other kinds of gel medium for other effects. The photo on page 118 shows mixed molding paste and paint for the covers. It dries to a slightly tacky finish. Another example is shown in Chapter 1, page 21.

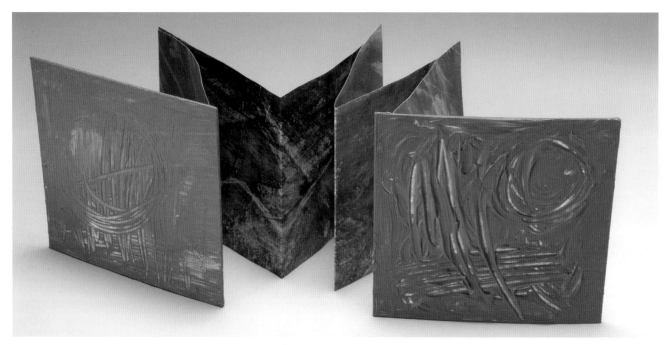

Techniques: texture paste, acrylic paints for the cover

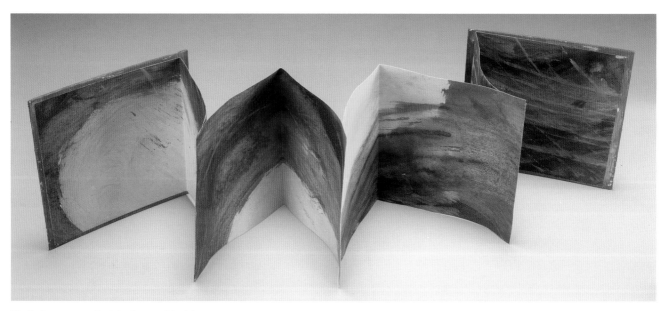

Techniques: acrylic inks layered inside

6 books & projects

***MESSAGE SEAT*, 2005;** acrylic ink, acrylic paints, gesso; circle accordion; 5½" × 6" (14 cm × 15.2 cm).
Techniques: multiple hand-cut stencils with Venetian red, black, and gold gesso; white stenciled rectangles, words written in black acrylic ink with a pointed round brush, brush-handle painting

ainted papers can be transformed into a variety of objects, such as books, cards, and boxes.

Not only does the paper change shape, but the look of the painting changes as well. We've discussed cutting the paper into small pieces, but choosing a sequence for the pages becomes an even more dynamic process. Rhythm is revealed in surprising ways.

Each of these nine projects is made with either heavyweight or textweight paper; some are painted only on one side and others on both sides. Projects that require painting on one side only appear first. For each three-dimensional project you will be shown a folding, sewing, or gluing process (or combination). Before beginning a project, review the Diagram Key on page 121, where you will find icons, dotted lines, and other clues to how the diagrams indicate steps for folding and binding.

Certain tools make book construction easier. A bone folder is handy for scoring lines where the paper is to be folded and is useful for smoothing the paper into a tight crease after each fold is formed. Linen thread is a good choice for sewing, although any thread that does not break or stretch easily works well. A metal ruler, a sharp pencil, and a sharp art knife are also tools that will help you.

To hold your projects together securely, use PVA, an archival white glue. For large applications, pour some glue on a paper plate and use an inexpensive brush to apply the glue to your project. Choose the

***ABOVE/UNDER*, 2005;** acrylic inks, gesso, graphite; circle accordion; 5 ½" × 6" (12.8 cm × 15.2 cm).

Techniques: acrylic ink applied with various brushes, gesso, pencil, acrylic ink lettering applied with a crowquill pen

brush size according to the size of your project, using a large brush when you need to apply glue to large areas and a smaller one when working on more defined areas. For smaller projects, you may also use a piece of cardboard to spread the glue. A brush will give you more control, and you will be able to spread the glue more evenly, but you will also need to wash it out thoroughly when you are finished. Many people like using the cardboard, if only because they can throw it away when they are through. Heavy acrylic gel medium is an alternative to PVA and works just as well, sometimes better, especially when both sides of the paper have been painted, since it is formulated to be compatible with all acrylic media.

For best results, make sure that all your papers and boards are cut so that the grain is going in the same direction when they are folded or glued together. To easily observe paper-grain direction, tear an article out of the newspaper; you'll notice that one edge is ragged, one tears straight. The straight edge is "with the grain," the ragged edge is "against the grain." If you are making a book structure, the paper should always be oriented so that the grain is parallel to the spine of the book. Test the grain of a piece of paper by gently bending the paper, as if you were attempting to fold it in half. Don't actually crease it; you are just testing for resistance. Try one direction, then the other. As you try to bend the paper you will find that one way seems easier. The grain runs parallel to this easier fold. For bookmaking, "grained short" means that the paper is cut so the grain runs parallel to the shortest side. "Grained long" means that the paper is cut so the grain runs parallel to the longest side. Short and long are indicated for each paper in the projects. More detailed bookmaking techniques may be found in my book *Creating Handmade Books*.

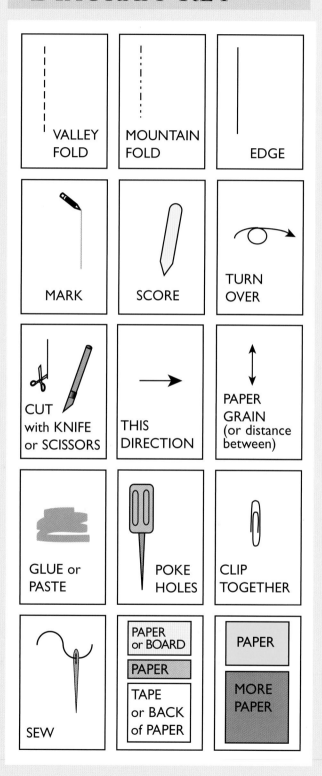

DIAGRAM KEY

VALLEY FOLD

MOUNTAIN FOLD

EDGE

MARK

SCORE

TURN OVER

CUT with KNIFE or SCISSORS

THIS DIRECTION

PAPER GRAIN (or distance between)

GLUE or PASTE

POKE HOLES

CLIP TOGETHER

SEW

PAPER or BOARD

PAPER

TAPE or BACK of PAPER

PAPER

MORE PAPER

BOOKMAKING TOOLS

While each project lists the specific tools and materials needed, you may wish to keep the following bookmaking items handy. Tools are listed by use and category. You can get them at most art-supply stores.

PENCIL. Any kind. Sharp is best so that you can measure and mark accurately. A thick mark will yield imprecise results.

BONE FOLDER. This tool, made of smooth bone and often pointed at one end and rounded at the other, is used for scoring paper and for creasing. Any size will work.

METAL RULER. For measuring and to use as a guide for your art knife, when cutting, or bone folder when scoring a fold line. A 12" (30 cm) ruler is fine for normal use. A 24" (60 cm) ruler is handy for cutting large papers.

ART KNIFE AND SELF-HEALING CUTTING MAT. I prefer a #1 X-Acto knife with #11 blades. A sharp knife gives best results, so keep spare blades on hand and change them often. You need to change the blade when you hear the tip chip off or if you look closely at the end and see that it is flat and no longer pointed. A cutting mat protects the surface on which you are working and may also lengthen the life of your blade. A 9" x 12" (approximately 22 cm x 30 cm) mat is good for small projects. An 18" x 24" (approximately 45 cm x 60 cm) mat is great when cutting large papers and boards.

PAPER CUTTER. A paper cutter is a quick and accurate alternative to measuring with a ruler and then cutting with a knife and cutting mat; to work well, the blade must be at least as long as the longest edge you are cutting. (See "metal ruler," above, for size recommendations.)

SCISSORS. Sharp scissors work best for cutting cords, linen tape, and corners.

SELF-ADHESIVE LINEN TAPE. For joining abutted pages. You can find this tape at most art-supply stores, shelved with other bookbinding or framing materials. The only brand I currently know of is Lineco. Make sure it is self-adhesive (sticky back) and not gummed (which you would have to wet). Also make sure it is linen, which is flexible, and not paper, which is stiff. I've only ever seen this particular linen tape 1¼" wide (3.2 cm).

PVA (POLYVINYL ACETATE) GLUE. An archival white glue. The small bottle works as an applicator, but for best results on larger areas, decant the glue onto a paper plate so you have more control when applying it with a brush or piece of cardboard.

PAINTBRUSH. For applying glue. You can use a stencil brush or any other brush with synthetic bristles. You can also use small pieces of cardboard.

MAGAZINES OR CATALOGS. Discarded glossy magazines and catalogs are ideal for protecting the surface on which you are working. Open one to the centerfold, remove any staples, if present, and start gluing your project there. Whenever you get glue on the page, fold it over or crumple it up and discard it. This way you can protect your project from inadvertently being dipped in glue. Newspaper is not a good alternative because the ink may transfer to your project and the paper itself is too absorbent.

CORNER ROUNDER. This paper punch is optional but nice to use. It is made of plastic and metal. You insert the corner of a piece of paper into it and press down. The punch clips off the edge, leaving a rounded corner.

Techniques: acrylic inks applied with various brushes, paste papers, faux marble, granite

Tools: art knife and cutting mat or a paper cutter (if your paper is not already cut to size); bone folder (optional)

Materials

Rectangle of textweight or heavyweight paper, four times as wide as it is tall (4:1), grained short, painted on one side

Example Size

This square envelope can be any size you desire. Begin with a rectangle of paper whose smaller dimension is the size you want the sides of the folded square to be.

Origami Envelope
(one-sided)

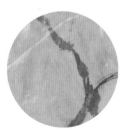

Make this square envelope and put a card, tag, tiny book, or small shikishi (a Japanese art board: see the project on page 136) inside. For the envelope, no adhesive or sewing is necessary, you simply fold the paper as shown.

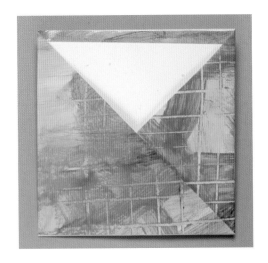

1. If necessary, cut the paper to the desired size. Place the paper, painted-side down, horizontally on a work surface. Fold the paper in half, aligning the left edge with the right edge.

2. Fold the top layer back to the left, aligning the edge with the first fold.

3. Open both folds so the paper is flat. Fold the right edge to the center. Then open the paper and keep it oriented as shown.

4. Fold the square section at the right edge of the paper in half diagonally, bringing the top right corner across and down.

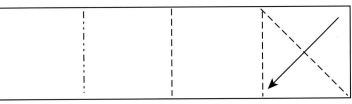

1

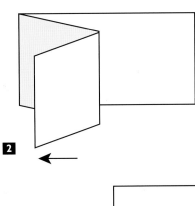

2

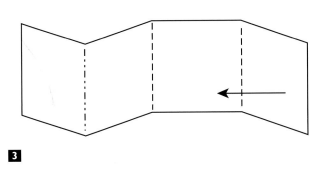

3

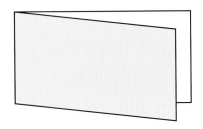

4

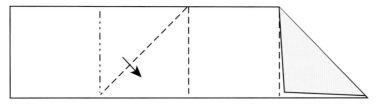

5

5. Fold the second square section from the left in half diagonally, bringing the left edge across and down.

6. Fold up the square section now on the lower left, covering the triangular section made in Step 5.

7. Hold the left square section and the triangular section beneath it together; fold them as one onto the center square section.

8. To finish the envelope, tuck the right triangle behind the left folded triangle If the triangle doesn't fit neatly, open the project and adjust the folds so they are aligned.

9. The completed envelope.

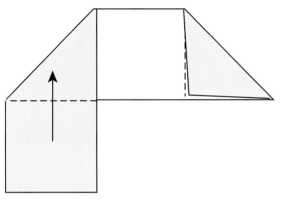

6

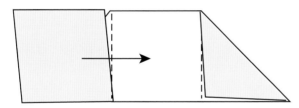

7

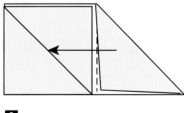

8

9

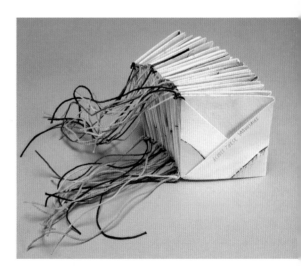

ACROSS THESE MOUNTAINS, 2007; acrylic inks, linen thread, book cloth; 2" × 2" × 2" (5.1 cm × 5.1 cm × 5.1 cm) origami envelopes bound into book form **Techniques:** drawing with dropper, wash, wet-on-wet

THE SEEKER, 2005; acrylic ink, gesso; circle accordion, 5½" × 6" (14 cm × 15.2 cm).

Techniques: acrylic inks applied with various brushes, Ebony pencil, stencil with gesso, red acrylic paint, handwriting in white and black inks with crow quill pen

Tools: pencil; 24" (61 cm) metal ruler; art knife and cutting mat (or 24" [61 cm] paper cutter), bone folder

Materials

One 22" × 30" (55.9 cm × 76.2 cm) sheet of printmaking or drawing paper, grained long, painted on one side

Five 6" (15.2 cm) lengths of self-adhesive linen tape

Example Size

5¼" × 6" (13.3 cm × 15.2 cm) book

Circle Accordion Book (one-sided)

By cutting a large piece of paper that has been painted on only one side, you can make a quick book with its own wrapper. All you need to add is some self-adhesive linen tape, which you can find at most art-supply stores. When ready to use the tape, bend up one corner of the backing so it will peel off easily.

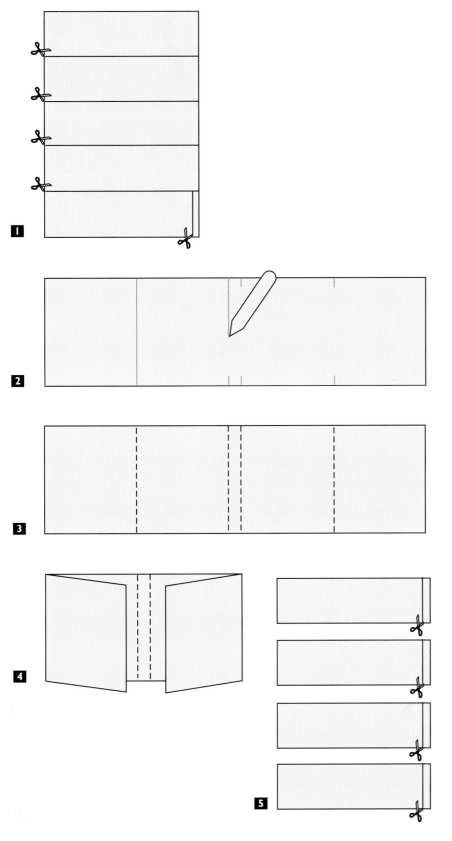

1. Using the pencil and ruler, divide the paper into five 6" × 22" (15.2 cm × 55.9 cm) strips, grained short. Cut the strips apart, using the ruler to guide the knife. Select one strip of paper to be the cover of your book. Cut ½" (1.3 cm) from one end, making it 6" × 21½" (15.2 cm × 54.6 cm).

2. Place the cover strip, painted-side down, horizontally on your work surface. Measure and mark the top and bottom edges 5¼" (13.3 cm) and 10½" (26.7 cm) from the right and left ends. Using the bone folder guided by the ruler, score lines from top to bottom to connect each set of marks.

3. Fold the paper up along each of the two middle scores to create the spine. Open and flatten these two valley folds.

4. Align the left edge of the paper with the left edge of the spine, folding on the score made in Step 2. Fold the right edge of the paper in the same way, aligning it with the right edge of the spine.

5. Cut 1" (2.5 cm) from one end of each of the four remaining strips, so that each one is 6" × 21" (15.2 cm × 53.4 cm).

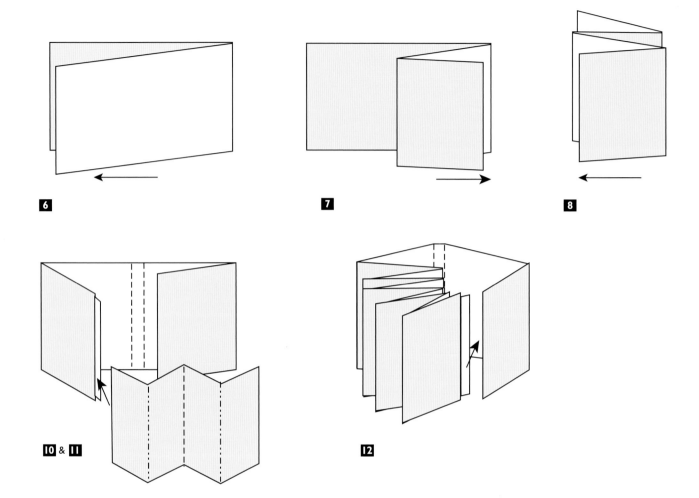

6. Place one of the remaining strips, painted-side up, horizontally on your work surface. Fold it in half, aligning the right edge with the left edge.

7. Fold the top layer back to the right, aligning the edge with the first fold.

8. Turn the paper over and fold back the layer now on top, aligning the edge with the first fold.

9. Repeat Steps 6 to 8 with the remaining three strips.

10. Make sure the pieces of linen tape are the same length or slightly shorter than the height of the cover; trim them if necessary.

11. Position the book cover on your work surface with the unpainted side of the spine facing up and the flaps folded in. Remove the backing from one piece of tape. Center the tape along the left edge

of the cover, adhering it to the unpainted side of the paper and making sure it extends beyond the edge. Select one of the folded pages to be first in the book. Align it, painted-side up, next to the edge of the cover with the tape, and press it against the tape to adhere.

12. Continue in this way to tape and attach the remaining pages. Fold up the back cover and tape the right edge of the last page to it in the same manner.

Variation: Cut the original paper into four equal strips for the book pages. Using a piece of black or a different decorated paper for the cover strip, cut it ¼" to ½" (6 mm to 13 mm) longer than the four strips. Measure the depth of the spine (all the strips folded and stacked, one atop the next) to determine how much longer the cover should be. This additional length allows for the depth of the spine, which may be different from the instructions given above.

LITTLE HILL, **2006;** acrylic ink, black gesso, circle accordion, 5" × 7" (12.7 cm × 17.8 cm).
Techniques: acrylic inks applied with various brushes, artist's tape mask, dropper and dry brush, stencil with black gesso

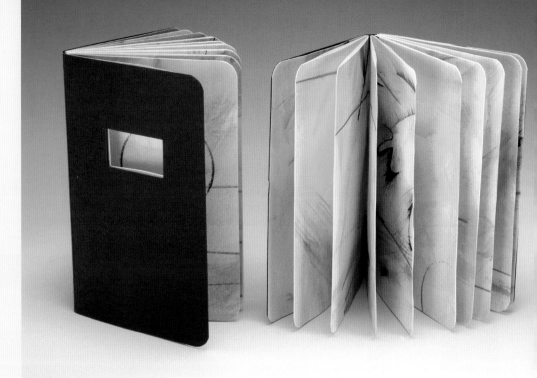

Techniques: acrylic ink wash, Ebony pencil, cup base dipped in acrylic ink

Tools: pencil; 24" (61 cm) metal ruler; art knife and cutting mat (or 24" [61 cm] paper cutter); bone folder; PVA glue in a squeeze bottle; scrap paper for template for a cover window (optional); large corner rounder (optional)

Materials

Textweight paper, approximately 19" × 25" (48.3 cm × 63.5 cm), no smaller than 18" × 24" (45.7 cm × 61 cm), preferably grained short, painted on one side

Heavyweight paper for the cover, 8⅜" × 6" (21.3 cm × 15.2 cm), grained short, plain or painted

Example Size

4" × 6" (10.2 cm × 15.2 cm) book

Album Accordion Book (one-sided)

The album accordion takes its name from a construction method described in the classic, Japanese *Bookbinding: Instructions from a Master Craftsman* by Kojiro Ikegami. It consists of several folded pages that are glued together at the fore edge (in this case, a loose vertical edge). This version of an accordion allows you to rearrange the order of the pages, add pages from other sources, or discard pages before you bind the book. If you are using scans of your painted paper to make several identical copies of a book, this structure works well because two pages will fit on a standard piece of laser printer paper. A corner rounder is not necessary but it gives the book a finished appearance.

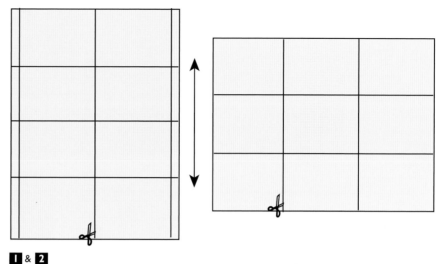

1 & **2**

Corner Rounder

1. Using the pencil and ruler, divide the painted paper into 6" × 8" (15.2 cm × 20.3 cm) rectangles, all grained short. Depending on the grain of the original sheet, you'll have eight or nine rectangles, as shown.

2. Cut the rectangles apart, using the ruler to guide the knife.

3. For the book pages, fold each rectangle in half with the painted side in, aligning the 6" (15.2 cm) edges.

4. Aligning the folds on the left, stack the pages one atop the other, in whatever order you like.

5. You'll assemble the book from back to front, so now turn the stack of pages over on your work surface, aligning the folds on the right.

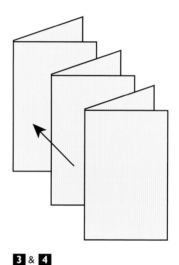

3 & **4**

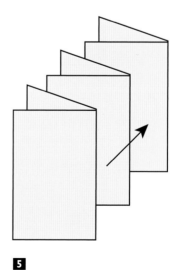

5

6. Flip the last folded page (the one on the top of the stack) over onto the work surface so its fold is on the left. Using PVA in a squeeze bottle, and holding the nozzle tightly against the paper, draw a line of glue along the right (fore) edge of the paper. Place the glue about ⅛" (3 mm) from the edge, starting and stopping about ⅛" (3 mm) from the top and bottom; this allows space for the glue to expand when you press another paper down on top of it.

7. Flip the next page on the stack over onto the glued page, aligning their folds. Using the bone folder or clean fingers, press the pages together along the glued edge. By aligning the folds you'll have the option of trimming the fore edges of the pages later.

8. In this manner, position and attach each of the remaining pages. If necessary, trim the fore edges so they are even. Always use the ruler as a guide and cut against it; don't try to do this freehand. You can measure and trim each set of pages separately or trim the whole stack of pages at once. If you are trimming the whole stack, you may need to make multiple cuts to get all the way through.

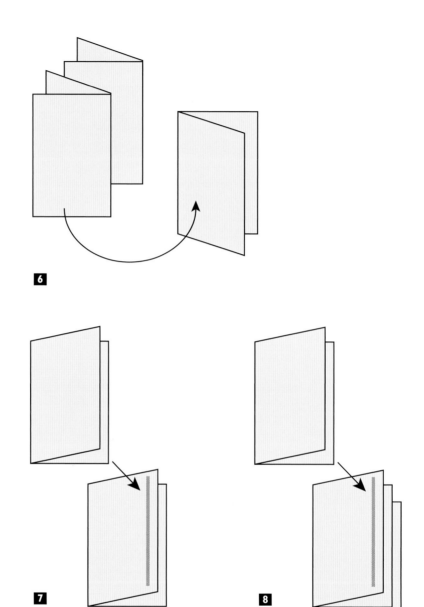

Folding and Attaching the Cover

9. Place the paper for the cover, painted-side down if the sides are different, horizontally on your work surface. Measure and mark the top and bottom edges 4" (10.2 cm) from each end. Using the bone folder guided by the ruler, score lines from the top to bottom to connect each set of marks.

10. Fold the paper up along each of the scores to create the spine, which will hold the folded edges of the pages.

11. Place the glued-together pages on your work surface with the folded edges to the left.
Apply glue to the fore edge of the top page. Insert the pages into the cover, sliding the folds against the spine and aligning the edges; press the cover down onto the glue for about 20 seconds to make sure it adheres.

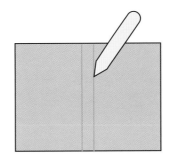

9

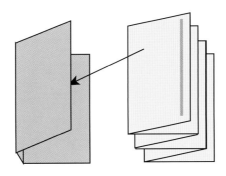

10 & **11**

12

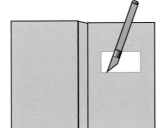

13

12. Turn the book over. Open the back cover. Apply glue to the fore edge of the last page. Close the cover and press it onto the glue for about 20 seconds. For best results, interleave sheets of waxed paper between the pages and put the book under a dictionary or other heavy book for a few hours or even overnight. The waxed paper will keep the pages separated and clean until the glue dries.

13. If you wish to create a window in the front cover, decide on a shape and make a template for it. Open the book and place it on the cutting mat so that the front cover is face up and all the free pages are under the back cover. Draw around your template to mark the shape of the window on the front cover. Cut out the window using the knife.

14. If you like, use the corner rounder to punch the corners on all the pages, one page at a time, and on the cover; you can see the corner rounder in the photo on page 131.

Variation: Instead of gluing the fore edges together in Step 6, use strips of painted paper (grained long) as used in the book *Start with Pencil*, or attach the fore edges with threads like *Driftwood & Roots* (page 9).

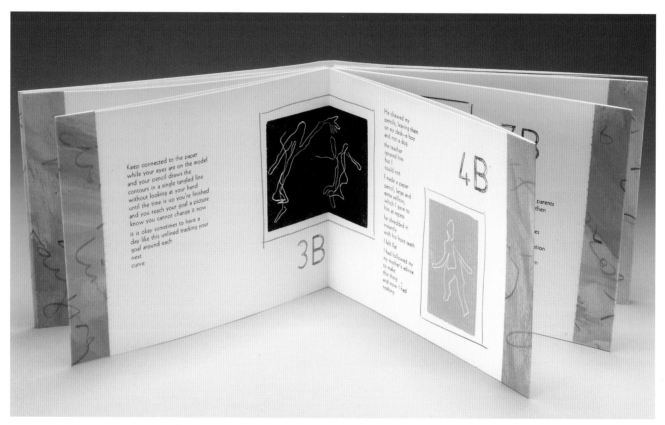

***START WITH PENCIL*, 2005;** acrylic inks, graphite, letterpress, linoleum cuts; album accordion with tabbed pages; edition of 45; 8" × 6" (20.3 cm × 15.2 cm). Techniques: acrylic ink wash, pencil

THE BLUE BRANCH, 2006; acrylic inks, graphite; album accordion; 4" × 6" (10.2 cm × 15.2 cm).
Techniques: multicolored droppers and dry brush, handwritten text applied with
ink and crow quill pen.

Techniques: dropper and dry brush, gold splatters

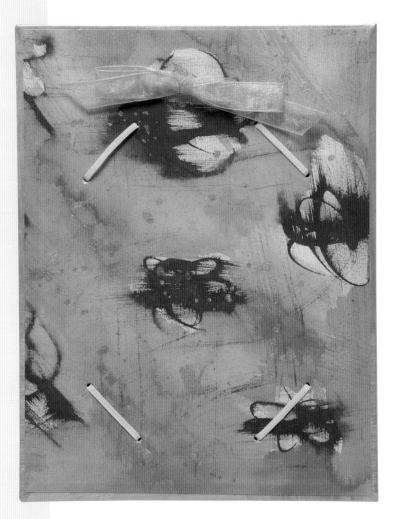

Tools: ruler, art knife and cutting mat; PVA glue; inexpensive brush for gluing; paper plate to hold the glue; pencil; scissors; magazines for scrap paper; bone folder; corrugated cardboard or stiff board to protect work surface when punching holes; awl or Japanese screw punch; large-eyed hand-sewing needle for the elastic

Materials

For all the example sizes below, use four-ply museum board, book board, or another stiff cardboard that is approximately $\frac{1}{16}$" (2 mm) thick for the base; lightweight paper painted with gold gesso or gold acrylic paint to bind the edges; decorated or plain lightweight paper to cover the front and back of the base.

Example Sizes

shikishi: $9\frac{1}{2}$" × $10\frac{3}{4}$" (24.1 cm × 27. 3 cm)
shikishi holder: 13" × 15" (33 cm × 38 cm)
postcard holder: 7" × 9" (18 cm × 23 cm)

Shikishi Materials

Four-ply museum board or book board, $9\frac{1}{2}$" × $10\frac{3}{4}$" (24.1 cm × 27.3 cm), grained long
Four strips of gold paper: two $9\frac{3}{4}$" × 1" (24.8 cm × 2.5 cm), grained short; two $10\frac{3}{4}$" × 1" (27.3 cm × 2.5 cm), grained long

(*continued on next page*)

Shikishi and Holder
(one-sided)

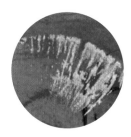

In Japan, there is a tradition of giving gifts of artwork, such as calligraphy or watercolor paintings, as a symbol of friendship and for special events like festivals, weddings, and the changing of the seasons. The art or writing is usually made on high-quality Japanese paper, such as Hosho, and is adhered to a board that has gold paper strips wrapped around the edges. Mounted this way it is referred to as *shikishi*. The shikishi is usually presented wrapped, although first it may be put into a hanging holder or frame (*shikishikake*), which is made from board and usually covered in silk brocade or another luxurious cloth. The frame includes elastic corner holders so that the art display can be changed easily; this is assuming you will be receiving or creating these regularly. This method of presenting artwork is the modern and more popular equivalent of presenting a scroll. Many shikishi resources are available online.

You can make your own version of the shikishi and its accompanying frame in an Asian or Western style. The technique used to wrap the boards is very similar to other bookbinding techniques. The usual size is approximately $10^{3/4}$" × $9^{1/2}$" (27.3 cm × 24.1 cm). One of these examples is for a smaller version that can hold standard size postcards in a vertical format.

Museum board, used for the base of each piece, is made from 100% cotton fibers and accepts ink and paint readily. For a variation of this project, you can make the shikishi and holder from painted boards. Follow the instructions for the shikishi to Step 11. End there or continue with Step 16 if you want to make it into a holder.

The shikishi and its holder and the postcard holder are made in the same way through Step 15; the only difference is their size and materials.

(*continued from previous page*)

Optional

Hosho or lightweight white paper for front (with or without completed artwork or poem), $9^{1/4}$" × $10^{1/2}$" (23.5 cm × 26.7 cm), grained long

White or decorative lightweight paper for back, $9^{1/4}$" × $10^{1/2}$" (23.5 cm × 26.7 cm), grained long

Shikishi Holder Materials

Four-ply museum board or book board, 13" × 15" (33 cm × 38 cm), grained long

Four strips of gold paper: two $13^{1/4}$" × 1" (33.7 cm × 2.5 cm), grained short; two 15" × 1" (38 cm × 2.5 cm), grained long

Two pieces decorated lightweight paper (or one decorated piece for the front and one plain piece for the back): $12^{3/4}$" × $14^{3/4}$" (32.4 cm × 37.5 cm), grained long

White $1/8$" wide elastic × $9^{1/2}$" long (3 mm wide × 24.1 cm long)

Ribbon or decorative cord, 24" (61 cm) long, for the hanger

Tassel (optional)

Postcard or Photo Holder Materials

Four-ply museum board or book board: 7" × 9" (18 cm × 23 cm), grained long

Four strips of gold paper: two $7^{1/4}$" × 1" (18.4 cm × 2.5 cm), grained long; two 9" × 1" (22.9 cm × 2.5 cm), grained short

Two pieces of decorated lightweight paper (or one decorated piece for the front and one plain piece for the back): $6^{3/4}$" × $8^{3/4}$" (17.1 cm × 22.2 cm), grained long

White $1/8$" wide elastic × 5" long (3 mm wide × 12.7 cm long)

Ribbon or decorative cord, 24" (61 cm) long, for the hanger

Tassel (optional)

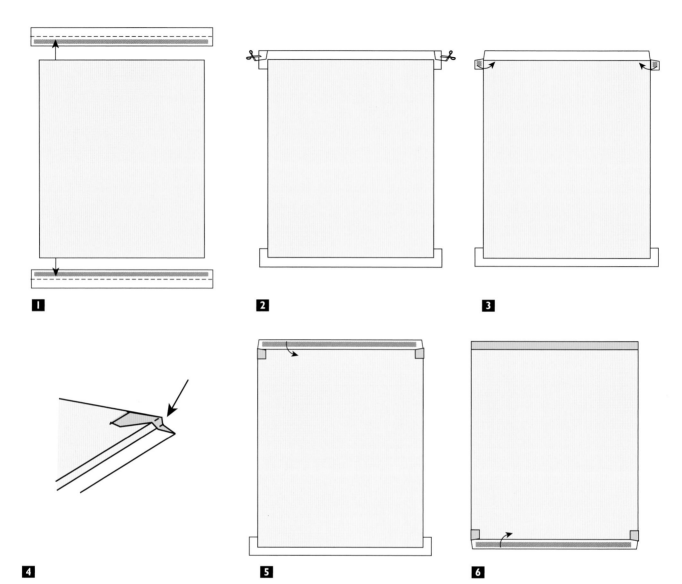

1   2   3

4   5   6

Making the Shikishi or Postcard and the Holders

1. Place the museum board vertically on your work surface. Fold each gold strip in half lengthwise, unpainted side in. Unfold one short strip and flatten it slightly; apply glue along one half of the strip and affix it, centered, under the top edge of the board, so the strip extends equally at both sides.

2. At the top of the board, draw a V-shaped line on each corner of the extending strip as shown; leave a little space between the board corner and the drawn line. Cut out the corners of the strip using a knife or scissors.

3. Apply glue to the extending ends of the strip and wrap them over the board.

4. Make sure the tips of the corners of the board are covered.

5. Apply glue to the rest of the extending strip and wrap it over the board.

6. Repeat Steps 2 through 5 at the bottom of the board.

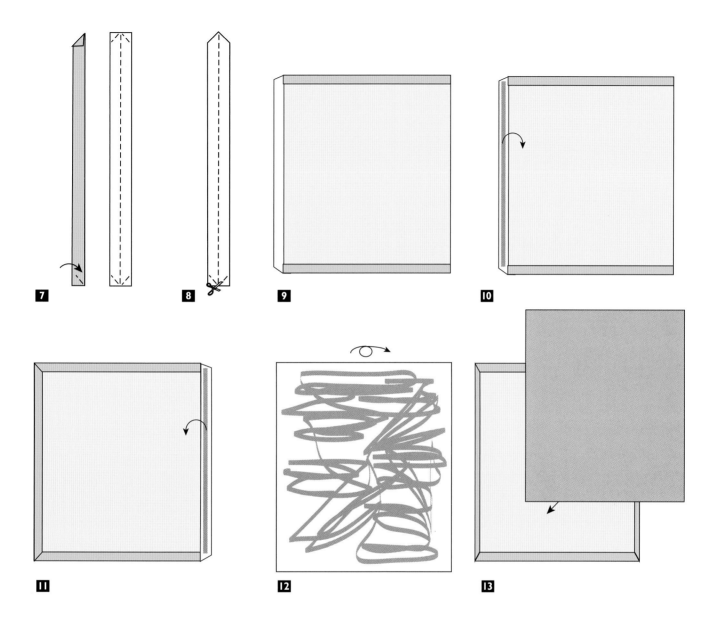

7. On each of the remaining gold strips, fold the corners up diagonally to meet the folded edge. Unfold.

8. Cut off each corner along the diagonal fold.

9. Apply glue along one half of one strip and affix it, centered, under the left edge of the board.

10. Apply glue to the rest of the extending strip and wrap it over the board.

11. Repeat Steps 9 and 10 to adhere the remaining strip to the right edge of the board.

12. Spread some magazines on the work surface to use as scrap paper. Put one piece of the lightweight

paper face down on the scrap paper. Use a brush and apply glue evenly across the surface. Pick up the sticky paper, turn it over, and hold it glue-side down.

13. Center the lightweight paper, glue-side down, on the gold-edged board. Smooth it over the board with clean hands or a bone folder.

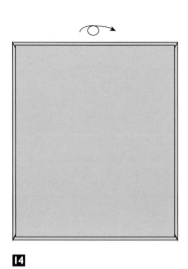

14

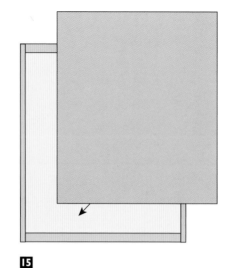

15

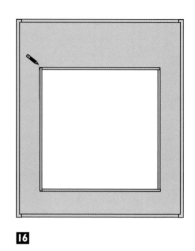

16

14. Turn the board over.

15. Repeat Steps 12 and 13 to cover the other side of the board with the second piece of lightweight paper. This is all you need for the shikishi; continue with Step 16 for the holder.

Completing the Holder

16. Place the holder board wrong-side up. Refer to the diagrams (16a

for the larger holder or 16b for the postcard holder) to see how much margin to allow on each edge. Place your shikishi or postcard on the board and draw around it with a pencil.

17. Remove the shikishi or postcard. Referring again to the diagram, mark the position of the holes for the hanging ribbon and

the elastic that will secure shikishi corners.

18. Place the holder on a work surface protected with cardboard. Using the awl or Japanese screw punch, poke a hole at each mark.

19. Cut the elastic into four equal pieces. Thread one onto the needle and sew from back to front

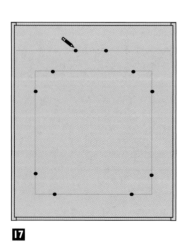

17

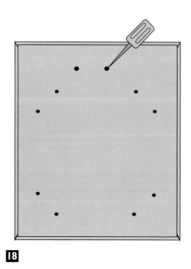

18

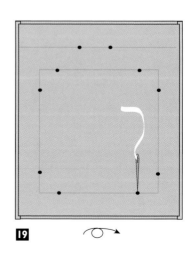

19

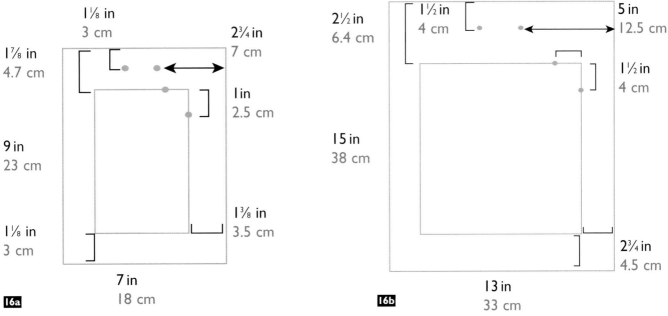

1⅛ in
3 cm

2¾ in
7 cm

1⅞ in
4.7 cm

1 in
2.5 cm

9 in
23 cm

1⅛ in
3 cm

1⅜ in
3.5 cm

7 in
18 cm

16a

2½ in
6.4 cm

1½ in
4 cm

5 in
12.5 cm

1½ in
4 cm

15 in
38 cm

2¾ in
4.5 cm

13 in
33 cm

16b

through one of the corner holes. Turn the board over.

20. From front to back sew the elastic through the corresponding corner hole. Remove the needle, leaving the loose ends of the elastic on the back of the board.

21. Thread a piece of elastic through each remaining pair of corner holes in the same way. Turn the board so the back is facing up.

22. Thread one end of the ribbon or cord from back to front through each of the top holes.

23. Tie the ends of each piece of elastic together. Turn the board over and tie a bow or knot in the ribbon. Pull the ribbon taut from the back. Slip the shikishi into the elastic corners.

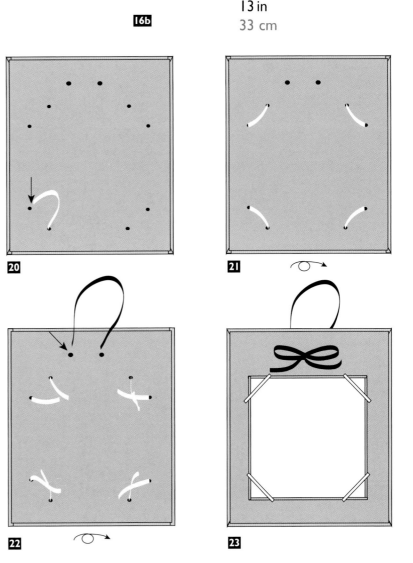

20

21

22

23

Variation: This variation on a shikishi uses just two pieces of lightweight paper to cover the board. One of them is large enough to cover the back of the board and wrap over its edges, taking the place of the separate strips of paper. If your larger piece of paper is gold, your covered board will look like shikishi from the front, but the back will be solid gold, with no border. You may also use this process to create a book cover.

A. Cut the larger piece of paper 1½" (3.8 cm) longer and wider than the board. Make sure the grain of the paper matches the grain of the board. Place the paper wrong-side up on your work surface. Center the board on it and draw around the board with a pencil.

B. Remove the board and apply glue to the paper inside the drawn rectangle.

C. Reposition the board on the paper and press it into place.

D. Cut off each corner of the backing paper on a diagonal, leaving a space equal to at least two

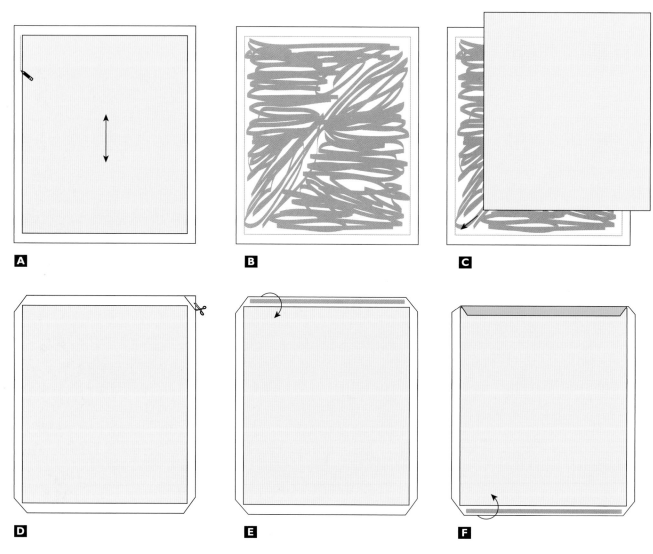

thicknesses of board between the very tip of the board and the cut.

E. Apply glue to the flap of paper extending along the top of the board, then wrap it over the edge.

F. Apply glue to the flap of paper extending along the bottom and wrap it over the edge.

G. Use your thumbnail to wrap the paper over the board at each corner. (See Step 4 page 138.) One edge at a time, glue and then wrap the flaps over the board.

H. Cut the smaller paper to be ½" (1.3 cm) shorter and ½" (1.3 cm) narrower than the board. Turn it wrong-side up, apply glue to it, and then invert it, center it on the board, and press it into place.

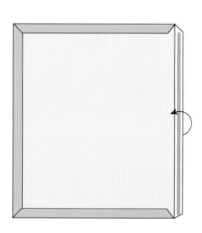

G

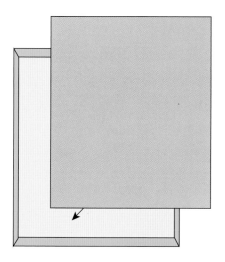

H

Techniques: acrylic ink wash, dropper and dry brush, fan brush dipped in gold gesso

Techniques: acrylic inks applied with various brushes, black gesso: sgraffito

Venetian Blind Book
(one-sided or two-sided)

Tools: bone folder; scissors; pencil; 12" (30 cm) ruler; awl or hole punch; cardboard to protect the work surface if using an awl

Materials

Both books: Cord or waxed linen thread, decorative bead for closure

Four-panel book: heavyweight paper 16" × 5" (40.6 cm × 12.7 cm), grained short, painted

Eight-panel book: heavyweight paper 16" × 2" (40.6 cm × 5.1 cm), grained short, painted

Example Sizes

Four-panel book: 4" × 5" (10.2 cm × 12.7 cm)

Eight-panel book: 2" × 2" (5.1 cm × 5.1 cm)

This is another version of an accordion book with the addition of a cord and bead to keep it closed. It does not require a cover and may be used as a card. Use a leftover piece of painted paper; add stenciled images, if you like. Instructions are given for both a four- and eight-panel version; you can use them as guides to make four- or eight-panel books in other dimensions as well. If you wish, add a small collage, stencil an image, or write a title on the front.

Making a Four-Panel Venetian Blind Book

1a. Choose one side of the paper to be the front. Place the paper, front-side down, horizontally on your work surface. Fold it in half, aligning the edges.

2a. Fold the top layer back to the right, aligning the end with the first fold.

3a. Turn the paper over. Fold back the layer now on top, aligning the end with the first fold. Continue with Step 6.

Making an Eight-Panel Venetian Blind Book

1b. Choose one side of the paper to be the front. Place the paper, front-side down, horizontally on your work surface. Fold the paper in half, aligning the edges.

2b. Unfold the paper. Fold each edge in, aligning it with the center fold. In origami this is called a cupboard because of its shape.

3b. Now fold each top section back, aligning the edges with the existing folds—like opening the shutters on a window. Turn the folded paper over.

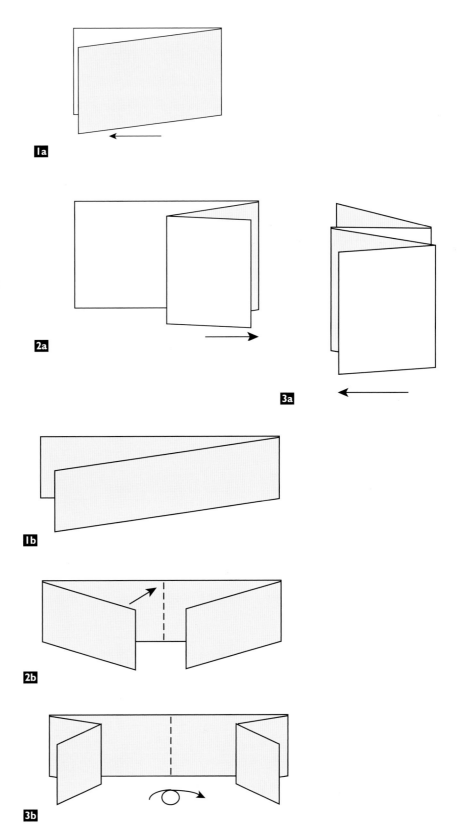

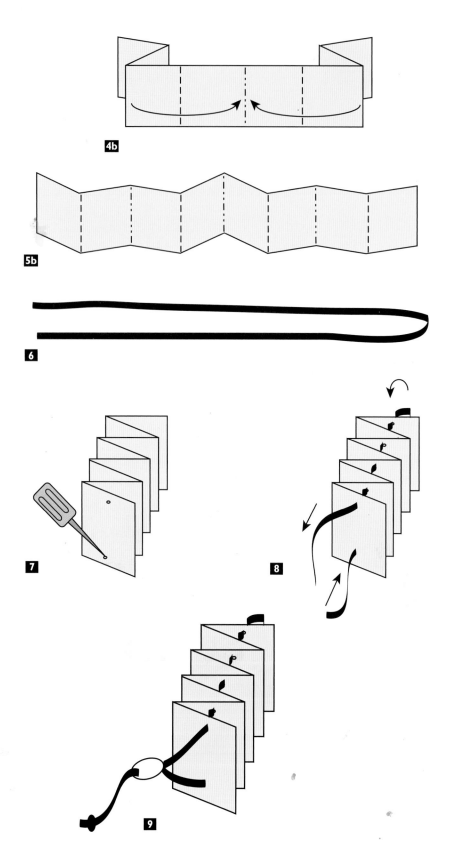

4b. Now it looks like a table. Fold the paper again, aligning the folded edges with the center fold.

5b. Unfold the paper. You should now have a fan fold with alternating valleys and mountains.

Adding the Cord and Bead

6. Cut a length of cord or waxed linen thread that is twice the length of the accordion when it is stretched out.

7. Fold the paper accordion again and place it on a work surface protected by thick cardboard. Measure and make a mark that is centered between the folds and ¼" (6 mm) below the top edge. Then measure and make a mark that is centered between the folds and ¼" (6 mm) above the bottom edge. Use an awl or screw punch to pierce a hole at each mark; be sure to pierce through all the layers.

8. Keep the accordion folded. Thread the cord from front to back through the bottom hole, take it up to the top hole, and thread it out to the front again; insert the cord into a large-eyed needle if it doesn't pass easily through the holes.

9. Twist the two ends of cord together and slide a bead over them. Tie the cords together in an overhand knot that sits about 1" (2.5 cm) from the ends. Add another knot if the hole in the bead is large.

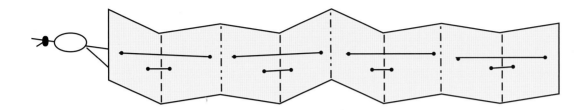

Note: To open the book, slide the bead to the knot and loosen the folds. To close the book, cinch the bead down so that it is resting securely on the front cover.

Variation 1: In Step 7, center the holes between the top and bottom, about ¼" (6 mm) from the folds on the right and left edges. This is how the black eight-panel accordion in the photo below is bound.

Variation 2: In Step 9, knot the cord ends individually so that the cord cannot slip through the punched holes in the book. Press the accordion closed and secure it by tying the cord ends in a bow. This is how the white accordion in the photo below is bound.

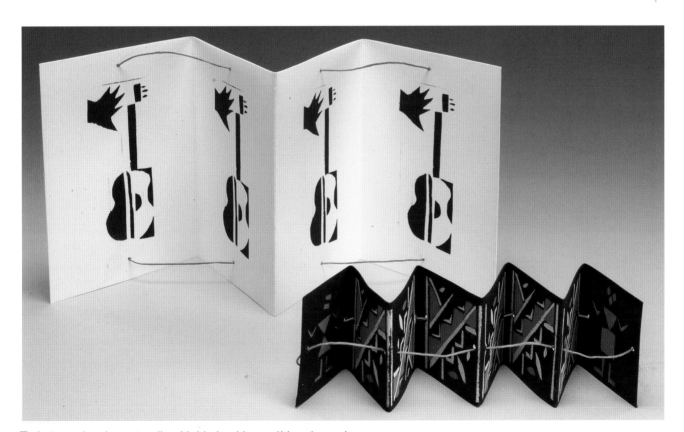

Techniques: hand-cut stencils with black, white, and Venetian red gesso

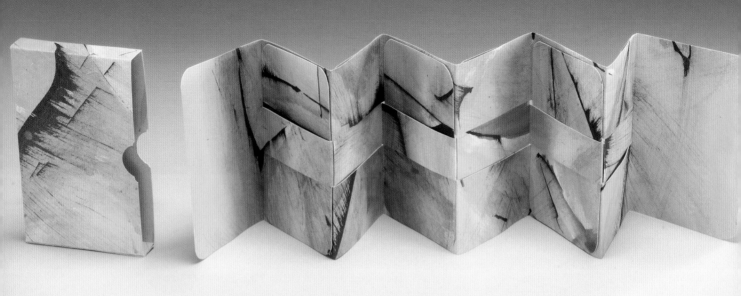

Technique: dropper and dry brush

Woven Accordion Book (two-sided)

Tools: pencil; 24" metal ruler (61 cm); art knife and cutting mat (or a 24" [61 cm] paper cutter); bone folder

Materials

One 22" × 30" (55.9 cm × 76.2 cm) piece of heavyweight paper, grained long, painted on both sides

Example Size

2¾" × 5" (7 cm × 12.7 cm) book

Bonnie Thompson Norman works full time for a commercial bindery, but evenings and weekends devises new bindings and teaches letterpress printing and book arts classes in her studio in Seattle, Washington. In 2002, Bonnie sent me a new book structure she designed. It is a Jacob's ladder made out of paper: a woven accordion. I sometimes refer to it as "Bonnie's Ladder." Sometime later, I realized that Ed Hutchins had sent me a version of this structure, but with many more slits, in 1999. To make it function, you have to separate the pages because they do not naturally drop open like the child's toy. Making one is easier than making the traditional toy; all you do is cut slits and weave cards. No adhesive, ribbon, or thread is necessary. An advantage to this structure is that you can arrange the cards until you get a pattern that you like. If you don't like one card, cut another from the extra scraps and reweave it. This structure changes the painted paper into a dynamic sculpture or interesting card. You will need to paint both sides of one large piece of heavyweight paper.

You will have enough paper to make a second book and a slipcase to hold each (see the photo at left) and the Paper Slipcase project on page 151. You could also make three smaller books and slipcases. See the note following the Woven Accordion Book directions for dimensions to cut the paper for other sizes.

Making the Accordion

1. Using the pencil, ruler, knife, and cutting mat, divide and then cut the paper into two 22" × 5" (55.9 cm × 12.7 cm) strips (these are now grained short); reserve the remaining paper for other projects.

2. Select one strip to make the accordion and choose one side to be the front. Place the strip, front-side down, horizontally on your work surface. Fold the strip in half, aligning the edges.

3. Unfold the strip. Fold each edge in, aligning it with the center fold. In origami, this is called a cupboard because of its shape.

4. Now fold each top section back, aligning the edges with the existing folds—like opening the shutters on a window. Turn the folded paper over.

5. Now it looks like a table. Fold the paper again, aligning the folded ends with the center fold.

6. Unfold the paper. You should now have a fan fold with alternating valleys and mountains.

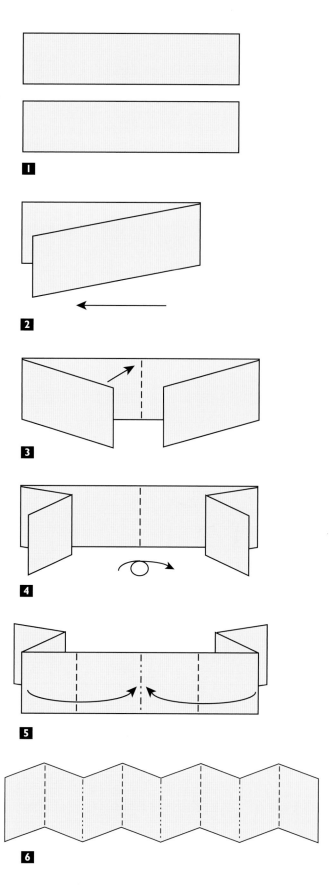

7. Unfold the accordion strip completely and flatten it, arranging it so there is a valley fold at each end; you should see three complete mountains. Measure and mark 2" (5 cm) from the top edge and 2" (5 cm) from the bottom edge on the valley fold at each end.

8. Place the flattened accordion on the cutting mat. Using the ruler to guide the knife and beginning and ending exactly on the outermost valley folds, cut a slit parallel to the top edge to connect the top marks. In the same way, cut another slit to connect the bottom marks.

9. Cut the second 22" × 5" (55.9 cm × 12.7 cm) strip of paper into eight 2⅝" × 5" (6.7 cm × 12.7 cm) cards (you need six cards for the project, but it's good to have choices).

Note: If your cards are too narrow they will fall out of the accordion. If they are too wide you will not be able to weave them into it. Allowing ⅛" (3 mm) difference between the width of the cards and the width of the accordion panels is sufficient and preferred.

Weaving the Cards

10. With the accordion still flattened and face up, lift the long center strip and slide one card under it; slide the card to the left, snug against the end of the slits.

11. Now hold down the long center strip and, starting from the back of the accordion, weave a card over it and out to the back again.

Make sure the card is snug against the first card.

12. Repeat the weaving process for the remaining cards, alternately inserting them under or over the center strip and tightening them as you go by sliding them over to the previous card. When you are finished, accordion-fold the book.

Note: To make three 2¾" × 4" (7 cm × 10.2 cm) books and three 2¾" × 4¼" × ½" (7 cm × 10.8 cm × 1.3 cm) slipcases out of one piece of paper, cut the size of the paper for the books to 22" × 4" (55.9 cm × 10.2 cm) and the size of the paper for the slipcase to 6" × 5¼" (15.2 cm × 13.3 cm), grained short.

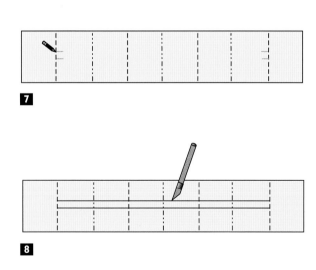

7

8

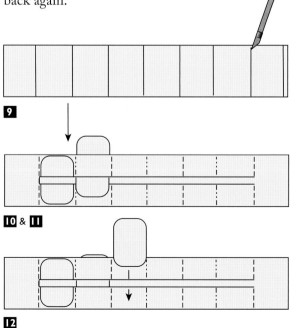

9

10 & 11

12

Techniques: acrylic ink wash, watercolor crayon applied to wet paper, dropper and dry brush

Paper Slipcase
(two-sided)

Tools: pencil; any size ruler; art knife and cutting mat or any size paper cutter; bone folder; small scissors; PVA glue; inexpensive brush or piece of cardboard for gluing; magazines for scrap paper

Materials

Heavyweight paper, painted on both sides (the paper left over from the Woven Accordion Book is sufficient)

Example Size

$2\frac{3}{4}$" × $5\frac{1}{4}$" × $\frac{1}{2}$" (7 cm × 13.3 cm × 1.3 cm)

A slipcase is a compact way to contain the Woven Accordion Book, to organize a set of cards, or to protect a stack of painted-paper samples. By making this open-ended box out of painted paper (especially one you've used for the book, cards, or samples) you can give the viewer a clue to what is inside.

It is easier to remove items from this kind of box if you make a thumbhole, otherwise you have to reach inside, possibly damaging the slipcase. You can trace around a penny for the half-circle thumbhole or create another shape. I like the thumbhole shown in Barbara Mauriello's book *Making Memory Boxes,* which is the half circle plus two little circles. Instead of the thumbhole, you may want to cut a large triangle at the edge of the slipcase. You can see that variation in the models on page 151.

Note: To change the size of this slipcase, start with the book you want to contain. For the projects in this book you can assume the depth is ½" (1.3 cm).

Paper width = (book width × 2) + depth

Paper height = book height + (depth × 2) + ¼" (6 mm)

1. Using the pencil, ruler, knife, and cutting mat, mark and then cut a paper rectangle 6" × 6½" (15.2 cm × 16.5 cm), grained long. If you are making a slipcase for a 2¾" × 4" (7 cm × 10.2 cm) book, use paper that is 6" × 5¾" (15.2 cm × 13.3 cm), grained short.

2. Place the paper vertically on your work surface (horizontally if you are making the small slipcase). It doesn't matter which side of the paper is up. Measure and mark ½" (1.3 cm) up from the bottom on the right and left edges.

3. Using the ruler to guide the bone folder, score a horizontal line to connect the marks.

4. Repeat Steps 2 and 3, this time measuring ½" (1.3 cm) down from the top.

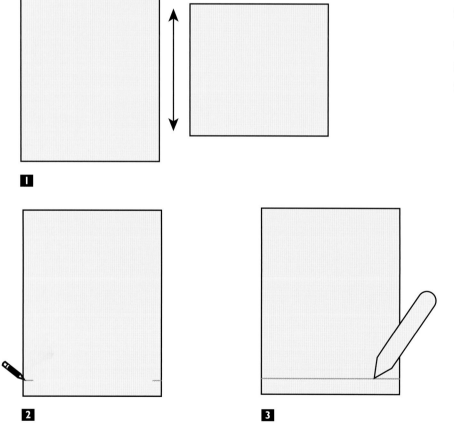

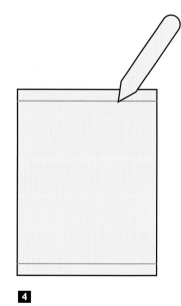

5. On the top edge, measure and mark 2¾" (7 cm) from the right edge (or measure the width of the book that will go inside the case). Measure and mark the same distance from the left edge. Repeat to measure and mark the bottom edge. Score lines from top to bottom to connect each pair of marks.

6. Using the knife, cut the scored line on each side of the center square in the top and bottom margin and then cut again at an angle to remove two notches inside each square; don't cut past the margin.

7. To make a template for the thumbhole, cut a rectangle of scrap paper with one side the same height as the slipcase paper. Fold this paper in half so it is half as tall as the slipcase paper.

8. At one edge of the fold, draw a shape half the size desired for the thumbhole. Using scissors or a knife, cut out the shape; discard the cutout.

9. Unfold the template. Align the template on one vertical edge of the slipcase paper. Use the pencil to draw the shape onto the slipcase.

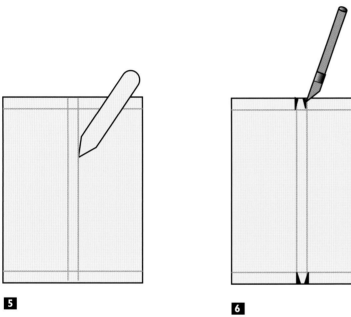

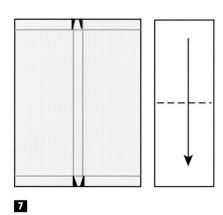

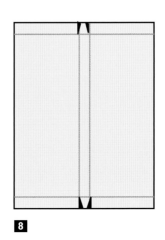

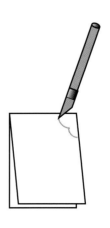

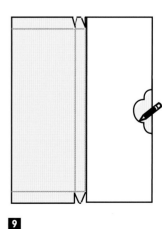

10. Cut out the shape using the knife or small scissors. Mark and cut another thumbhole in the opposite edge of the slipcase.

11. Choose one side of the paper for the inside of the slipcase and place that side up. Using the ruler as a guide, fold the paper up along each scored line.

12. At one end of the slipcase, apply a thin line of PVA to both sides of one of the flaps and to the outside of the little tab. Layer the flaps over the tab, placing the glued flap between the tab and the dry flap.

13. Holding the layers together, turn the slipcase so it rests it on the joined flaps. Make sure the edges are aligned at the open end. Rest a pencil horizontally inside the slipcase so that it touches the spine. Press down on the pencil to apply pressure evenly while the glue sets.

14. Repeat Steps 12 and 13 to glue the other end of the slipcase.

Variation: To make a double slipcase like the one on the top left of the photo on page 151, use paper that is twice as wide as the dimensions given at the beginning of the project (grained short). See the diagram for the placement of the score and cut lines. When you fold the slipcase, first fold it in half along the center score line with the inside facing out, then fold along all the other lines in the opposite direction, following Step 11 above. A triple slipcase will need paper three times as wide (grained short) and will have two mountain folds, such as the one used for the book *A Witness to Curious Speed* on page 100.

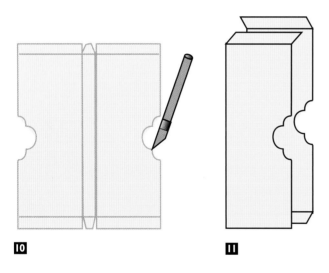

10   **11**

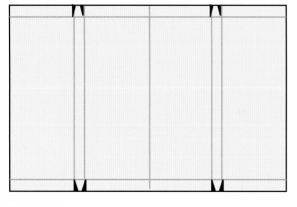

VARIATION

A WITNESS TO CURIOUS SPEED, **2005;**
detail of triple slipcase (full image on page 100)

Techniques: acrylic ink wash, hand-cut stencil with gesso

Tools: pencil; 18" (45.7 cm) metal ruler; art knife and cutting mat (or 24" [61 cm] paper cutter); bone folder; paper clips; corrugated cardboard or stiff board to protect your work surface when poking holes; awl; hand-sewing needle

Materials

Textweight paper for the interior pages: two pieces 18" × 16" (45.7 cm × 40.6 cm), grained long *or* one piece 18" × 24" (45.7 cm × 61 cm), grained short

Heavyweight paper for the wrapper: one piece 16¼" × 6⅛" (41.3 cm × 15.6 cm) grained short, painted on one side only or unpainted

Linen thread or other thread that will not stretch or break

Example Size

4" × 6" (10.2 cm × 15.2 cm) book

Two-as-One Book
(two-sided)

This book pairs the need for many pages with the ease of a simple binding. Use it for a short book of poems or quotations, an address book, or a colorful travel journal. You can do this even if you have never sewn before. For this example I used four painted pages from one large painted sheet and four painted pages from another so you could easily see how the book is put together. You can cut all eight pages from one single painted sheet of 18" × 24" (45.7 cm × 61 cm) textweight paper.

If you have some paper left over from the interior pages, use it to decorate the front of the wrapper, if you wish. When your book is assembled, you might want to draw on the pages with permanent pens or gel pens, write with a crow-quill pen dipped in ink, or add images using rubber stamps with a pigment-based inkpad.

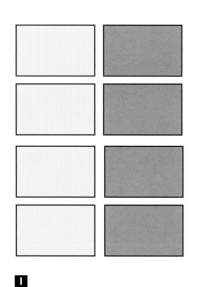

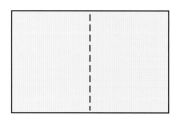

Making the Interior Pages

1. Using the pencil and ruler, divide the textweight paper into 8" × 6" (20.3 cm × 15.2 cm) grained-short pieces as follows: If you are starting with two smaller pieces of paper, divide each into six pieces. If you are starting with one large piece, divide it into nine pieces. No matter which size you start with, you need eight 8" × 6" (20.3 cm × 15.2 cm) pieces; set the extras aside for another project.

2. Fold each of the eight pieces in half, aligning the 6" (15.2 cm) edges.

3. Nest four of the folded papers together, one inside the other. Nest the other four papers together. You have made two signatures of four folded pieces each (or two eight-page signatures).

4. Arrange the two signatures back to back (with their mountain folds aligned).

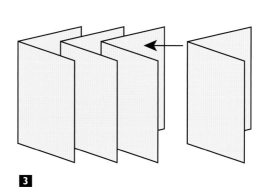

5. Hold the signatures together with paper clips at the top and bottom of the pages. Measure and mark the midpoint of the fold (3" [7.6 cm] from the top), and then mark two points equidistant from the first, placing them at least ¾" (1.9 cm) from the top and bottom edges. Place the book on a work surface protected with cardboard. Poke a hole at each mark with the awl.

6. Measure and cut a length of linen thread that is three times the height of your book, and thread the needle.

7. Sew with the needle through the center hole; it doesn't matter which side you start from. The diagram shows open pages that we will call the inside. Leave a tail of thread about 3" (7.6 cm) long inside.

8. From in to out, sew through the top hole.

9. From out to in, sew through the bottom hole (skipping the center hole).

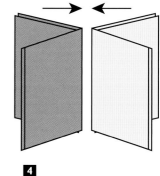

10. Finally, bring the needle back up through the center hole.

11. Arrange the loose thread ends so one is on each side of the long stitch. Tie the two ends over the long stitch in a square knot.

12. Trim the ends of the thread. Remove the paper clips. Find the two distinct signatures again, Hold one in each hand and begin gathering them back into their separate sections.

13. Close each signature.

14. Arrange the signatures so one sits on top of the other.

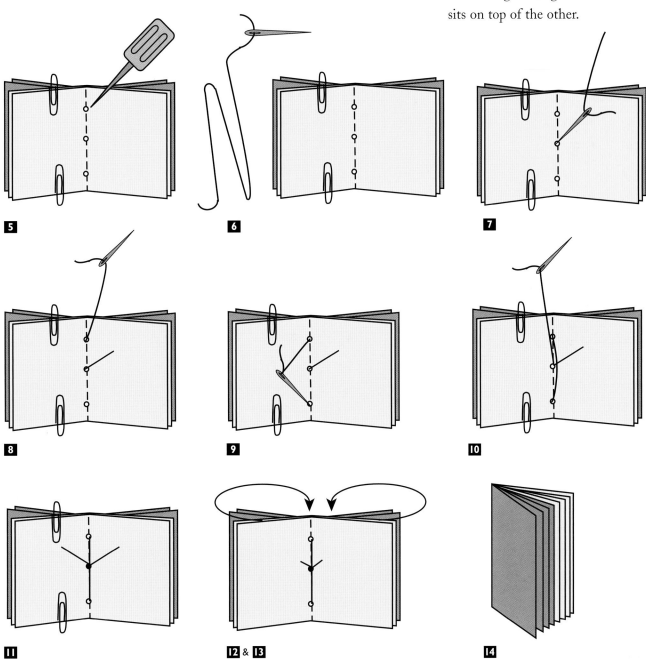

Making a Wrapper or Soft Cover

15. Place the heavyweight paper horizontally on your work surface. Measure and mark the midpoint of the top edge; then mark again ⅛" (3 mm) to each side of the first mark. Measure and mark the bottom edge in the same way.

16. Using the ruler to guide the bone folder, score a line to connect the top and bottom right-hand marks. Repeat for the left-hand marks. The space between the scored lines is the spine of the wrapper.

17. Fold up the left edge of the paper, aligning it with the scored line at the left edge of the spine.

Fold the right edge of the paper in the same way, aligning it with the right edge of the spine.

18. Place the book's interior pages (the text block) so that the sewn spine is aligned with the spine of the wrapper.

19. Wrap the cover flaps around the front and back pages of the book.

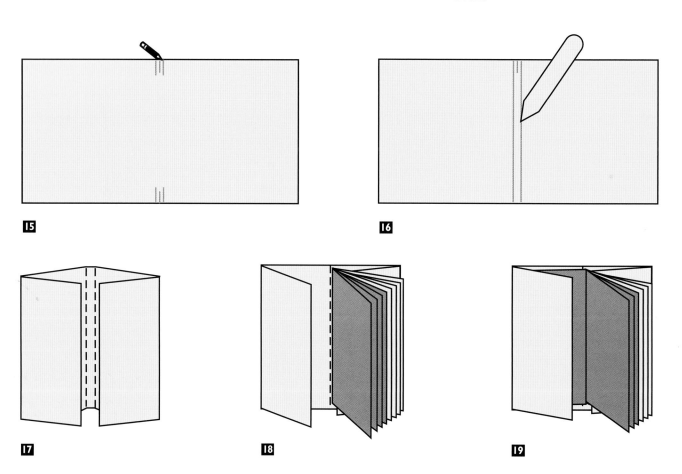

15

16

17

18

19

Technique: dropper and dry brush

Decorative Box
(two-sided)

Tools: pencil; 24" (61 cm) metal ruler; art knife and cutting mat (or 24" [61 cm] paper cutter); PVA glue; inexpensive brush or piece of board for spreading glue; magazines for scrap paper; awl or Japanese screw punch; corrugated cardboard or stiff board to protect your work surface

Materials

One 14" × 14" (35.6 cm × 35.6 cm) piece of four-ply museum board, painted on one side

Example Size

5" × 7" × 2" (12.7 cm × 17.8 cm × 5.1 cm)

This decorative box can be made and used in a variety of ways. Solid, it can be a sculpture. Add a hole to one of the boards before you assemble it and you can hang it on the wall. Make it a cube and fill it with beads, seeds, or beans for a shaker. For a shadow box, cut a window in it and put a picture inside before you seal the top. Museum board is made from 100% cotton fibers and accepts ink and paint readily. You can make this any size, just remember to trim ¼" (6 mm) from two opposite walls.

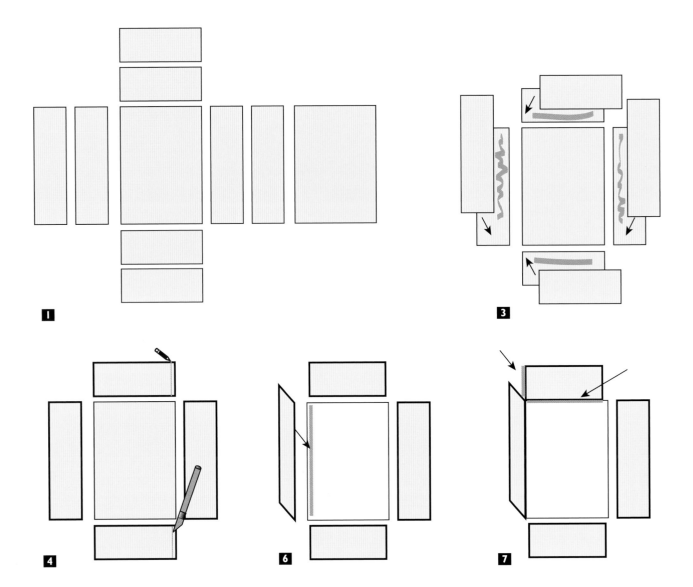

1. Using the pencil, ruler, art knife, and cutting mat, cut the board so you have two large boards 5" × 7" (12.7 cm × 17.8 cm), four side boards 2" × 7" (5.1 cm × 17.8 cm), and four end boards 2" × 5" (5.1 cm × 12.7 cm).

2. Paint the unpainted side of the two large boards with inks or paints. Let dry.

3. Apply PVA glue completely and evenly to the unpainted surface of the side and end boards. Adhere them in pairs, putting the glued surfaces together. Put them under a heavy book to dry for at least ten minutes, preferably an hour.

4. Measure and draw a line ¼" (6 mm) from one end (see diagram) of each 2" × 5" (5.1 cm × 12.7 cm) end board. Using the ruler to guide the knife along the line, trim ¼" (6 mm).

5. Place one of the large boards face down. If you want a window on the front, cut it now.

6. Arrange the side and end boards around the large board as shown. Apply glue to one long edge of one of the side boards and adhere it at a right angle on top of the large board; keep the sides and ends aligned. Hold in place for thirty seconds.

7. Apply glue to one short edge and one long edge of an end board.

8. Press into place perpendicular to the side board and large board, making sure it is aligned. Hold for thirty seconds.

9. Repeat Step 8 to glue and position the remaining side and end board.

10. If you wish to seal anything inside the box, add it now. If you want to hang the box, use the awl to punch a hole in the remaining large board, centering it roughly 1" (2.5 cm) below the top edge.

11. Apply glue to the top edges of all four side and end boards. Place the remaining large board on top; align the edges, and hold in place for at least one minute.

12. Put a piece of waxed paper over the box and place a light weight on it (a children's picture book or other large, thin book would be fine). Let dry for several hours or overnight.

Variation: For a tougher finish for box sides, or for painted boards for book covers, use acrylic paint mixed with paste, gesso, or gel medium rather than acrylic ink alone. Distress the boards first, if you like, by hammering textured metal objects into them. The covers of the books in the photograph have been painted with

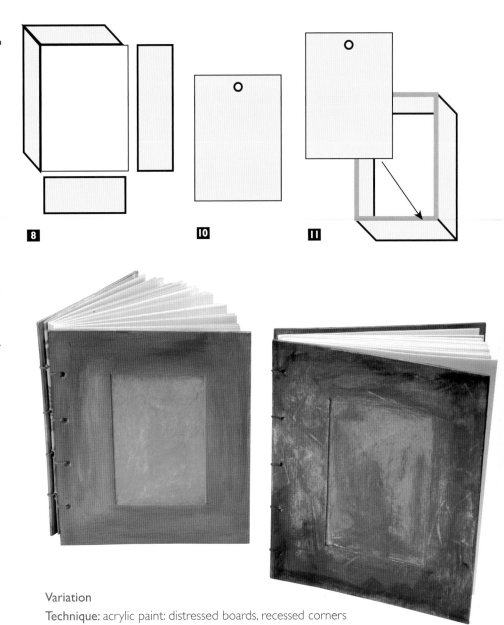

Variation
Technique: acrylic paint: distressed boards, recessed corners

acrylic paints and are lightly distressed. If the covers are made from four-ply board, it's easy to create a recessed shape like the rectangles on these. First, draw the shape you want the recess to be. Then, along the lines of the shape,

cut into the board about halfway. Use the tip of the knife to dig up two plies (layers) of the board; then peel out the shape. You can make recesses in your boxes or books to add dimension and a place to put a small picture, label, or title.

explorations

Just as it took you time to learn to spell and write your name, it will take time to internalize painting methods and be able to work on your own. Once you get a feel for how the materials work and how you like to work with them, your art will begin to reflect your personality and your own interests. Your painted papers will acquire a signature look, unique to you. Art is an expression, an interpretation of the world through your own eyes.

The enchanting surface can also be an invitation for a closer, deeper look. The different techniques focus primarily on surface colors and textures, but you can work on other levels as well. Working spontaneously, you can loosen up, work quickly, and enjoy moving color around; this way of working will show up in your painted paper as emotion and

THE DIVER, **2005;** acrylic inks, acrylic paint, gesso, watercolor crayons on paper; 22" x 30" (55.9 cm x 76.2 cm). Techniques: acrylic ink wash, watercolor crayon applied to wet paper, gesso, acrylic paint: sgraffito

movement—expression in a subconscious form. Another way to work is with intention. You may want your papers to have content or meaning based on an idea rather than on spontaneous feeling. In that case, you may want to add words or images to reinforce your idea as a conscious form of expression.

For a combined approach, try painting the paper spontaneously to start, then think consciously about it afterward, using it as a Rorschach test. Examine it to see what it reminds you of. At this point, add a literal message or tie it consciously to a theme. You might explore writing relevant phrases all over the paper or adding single words by hand with a pen dipped in ink, with alphabet stencils, or with rubber stamps. If the paper is then cut or folded and made into a book or card, the words will become mysteriously fragmented and partially concealed, adding another layer of meaning to your work.

Exploration is part of the process of making art. You can explore your emotional responses to colors and favorite subjects, and you can explore various physical materials, such as inks, paints, and gesso. By keeping your hands moving you open yourself to learning: this is what exploration is about. Wherever you begin, be open to chance occurrences and see where they lead you. As you explore, ask yourself what more you can bring to the paper and how can it evolve into something meaningful to you; something only you could have created.

ANTENNA, 2007; acrylic inks, gesso, book cloth, linen thread, sticks; 2" × 2" × 2¼" (5.1 cm × 5.1 cm × 5.7 cm) box (7" [7.8 cm] tall, including antenna), 1¾" × 1¾" × 1¾" (4.4 cm × 4.4 cm × 1.9 cm) album accordion. Techniques: masked and ink-painted squares, layered freehand forms, gesso and handcut stencil

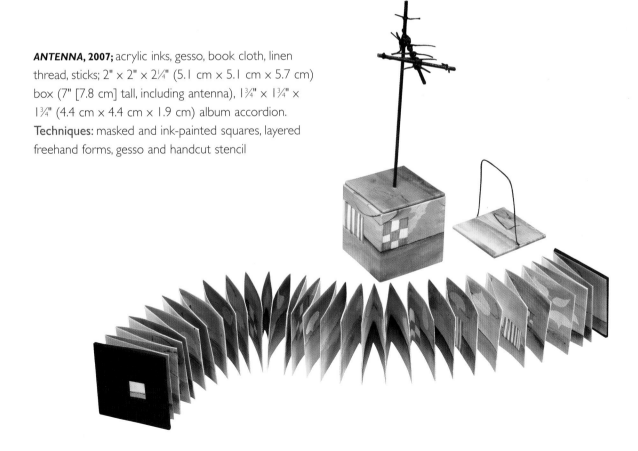

glossary

acrylic A type of plastic that becomes a carrier for paints, inks, adhesives, or other media.

archival This term is used loosely to mean materials that are acid-free and will remain stable over time. Acids cause paper to turn yellow or become spotty or brittle. Very high-quality materials may be buffered, which means they start out with a higher alkaline content; this helps them resist acids in the air or in on the skin. Since you'll be touching books and paper, acids in the skin—especially the hands—can be damaging to books and papers in the long run, so buffering is a definite advantage.

artist's tape A masking tape used to block areas from receiving paint or ink. Tape labeled "for paper" or "low tack" is best for the techniques in this book as it does not leave a residue or pull up fibers from the paper when removed. See also: mask/masking.

collage Two or more pieces of paper or objects that are glued together in a pleasing composition. The papers may also be arranged in a pattern.

crayons, watercolor Also called water-soluble crayons, these are crayons in which the pigment is suspended in a solid carrier and activated by water. Unlike wax crayons, these crayons dissolve in water. They will reactivate if they get wet, but a coating of acrylic ink or varnish will seal them permanently.

dry-brush technique Using undiluted ink or paint with a paintbrush that has not been dampened.

dye In papermaking and most artists' media, a plant-based coloring substance is usually referred to as a dye, and these substances are generally not lightfast. Dyes are soluble powders or begin as liquids.

faux finish A technique that mimics a texture such as marble, granite, or wood and may trick the eye into thinking the paper is of that material.

frottage A rubbing technique in which a piece of paper is placed over objects and then rubbed with color. For paste paper frottage, a mixture of paint and paste is first applied to the paper (paste paper), then a flat tool, such as a credit card or piece of cardboard, is scraped over the top, leaving the outlines of the hidden object visible on the paste paper.

gesso A chalky, toothy (somewhat rough), opaque, paintlike substance with a matte surface. It is usually made of calcium carbonate mixed with an acrylic polymer medium or other carrier. It looks like white paint. Originally, the calcium carbonate was mixed with rabbit-skin glue and used as a primer for canvas. All references to gesso in this book are to acrylic gesso.

glaze A thin layer of acrylic ink, diluted acrylic paint, or varnish used in multiple layers to build up the surface texture or color and add depth or shading.

ink, acrylic Pigment that is suspended in a liquid acrylic carrier. A characteristic of acrylic ink is that it can be diluted with water, cleaned up with water while wet, but dries to a permanent, unchangeable surface. You can apply one color, let it dry, then apply another color across it without either color changing. See also: opaque and translucent.

ink pencils This is a new product that is compatible with—and very effective with—papers that have been painted and are dry. Use the ink pencils in the same way you draw with other colored pencils. To activate the ink, wet a small brush and touch it lightly on the colored areas, one color at a time. Once the water dries, the color remains permanent.

layer/layering Putting one thing atop another, such as colors. Layering color adds depth to a design, making it more interesting to look at.

lightfast If a paper, ink, paint color, or stamp pad is labeled "lightfast" it means it should not fade rapidly in the light. Pigments are generally lightfast. Dyes are generally not.

markmaking A term used to describe a variety of ways to create texture, color, lines, patterns, movement, or shading that often employs a tool (such as a pencil, brush, stick, comb, or plate). The marks made may be decorative, representational, or abstract in effect, or a combination of these. Each person has her own style of making marks; a person's handwriting is a kind of personal markmaking. Markmaking is your artistic handwriting.

mask/masking A covering that prevents areas from receiving color. Masking media include artist's tape, liquid mask, and masking film. The liquid and film are often referred to by their brand name in the United States, for example, Frisket. The self-adhesive film can be cut into shapes and adhered to paper; the liquid may be brushed onto the paper directly. Painting is done over the mask, which then is removed to reveal the color of whatever was underneath it.

opaque A description of something that blocks light or color. Use an opaque paint or ink over other colors to cover them up—no color will show through. Opaque media are also good for adding text or imagery to a painted paper.

paint, acrylic Pigment that is suspended in a thick, acrylic carrier or emulsion. It may be purchased in tubes or jars for convenience. It is initially water-soluble but dries to a permanent, unalterable, mostly flexible, plasticlike finish.

paint, watercolor Color pigment that remains water soluble, even after it dries. Sometimes just called watercolors.

palette The dish that holds the colors while you are painting and also a selection of colors you might choose for a particular project.

paste paper A paper on which a mixture of paint and paste (such as wheat paste) is applied, then incised or scraped to create a pattern or texture for a decorative effect.

pattern/patterning An allover design that generally repeats in some way. Patterning is a copied motion.

pigment A mineral- or synthetic-based coloring substance relatively insoluble and that should remain permanent and lightfast.

pochoir An intricate hand-stenciling process characterized by crisp outlines. This process originated in France in the late 1800s. It involves using multiple stencils, one for each color. Pochoir and stenciling are terms used interchangeably today.

resist A bottom layer of color that repels a top layer; because the top layer can't adhere to it, the bottom color remains visible. Resists are permanent parts of your painting.

sgraffito Incising or scratching into a painted surface; a kind of markmaking.

signature Several sheets of paper that are folded in half and nested, one folded sheet inside another, their folds aligned.

stencil A flat object, usually paper, vellum, cardboard, or plastic, with one or more cutout holes. Paint or gesso is applied through the hole to paper placed underneath the stencil. Whatever shape was cut out of the stencil (the negative) becomes the image on the paper (the positive). The act of stenciling is the creation of this positive image; it is also called pochoir.

textweight Refers to a lightweight or medium-weight paper used as pages in a book such as this one.

translucent Able to be partially seen through; semi-transparent. Use thinned paint or transparent ink if you want the color of the paper to show through for an airy, open feeling, or use it on top of other colors to tint them or add depth.

wash Used as a noun to describe a technique where one color is applied in long, overlapping strokes to fill a large area. The paper is usually moistened first. The color can be mixed or diluted so that you have a sufficient amount to cover the paper.

about the author

Alisa Golden makes painted and letterpress printed books under the imprint she established in 1983, never mind the press. She is also the author of *Creating Handmade Books* (1998), *Unique Handmade Books* (2001), and *Expressive Handmade Books* (2005), all published by Sterling. She has a BFA in printmaking from California College of Arts and Crafts and currently teaches at California College of the Arts, San Francisco Art Institute, and the San Francisco Center for the Book. Her book art is collected by universities, libraries, and museums across the country and may also be seen at www.neverbook.com.

index